Collins
English for Exams

D0127819

Get Ready for IELTS
LISTENING

Jane Short

Collins

HarperCollins Publishers
77-85 Fulham Palace Road
Hammersmith
London W6 8JB

First edition 2012

Reprint 10 9 8 7 6 5 4 3 2 1

© HarperCollins Publishers 2012

ISBN 978–0–00–746062–5

Collins® is a registered trademark of HarperCollins
Publishers Limited

www.collinselt.com

A catalogue record for this book is available from the
British Library

Typeset in India by Aptara

Printed in China by South China Printing Co.

About the author
Jane Short has taught English as a second language and
English for academic purposes for over 30 years. She is
currently Director of Learning and Teaching for the Centre
for English and World Languages at the University of Kent.

Contents

Introduction

Who is this book for?

Get Ready for IELTS Listening has been written for learners with a band score of 3 or 4 who want to achieve a higher score. Using this book will help you improve your pre-intermediate listening skills for the IELTS Academic Listening test.

You can use *Get Ready for IELTS Listening*:

- as a self-study course. We recommend that you work systematically through the 12 units in order to benefit from its progressive structure.
- as a supplementary listening skills course for IELTS preparation classes. The book provides enough material for approximately 50 hours of classroom activity.

Get Ready for IELTS Listening

- This comprises a book and two CDs.
- The book contains **12 units**. Each unit focuses on a different topic and these topics are ones that often appear in the IELTS exam.
- After every three units, there is a **Review unit** which helps you to revise the language and skills covered in the previous units.
- At the end of the book the **Practice test** gives you the opportunity to take an IELTS-style test under test conditions.
- There is also a full **answer key** at the back of the book so you can check your answers. Here you will find suggested answers for more open-ended questions and model answers for the exam practice questions in Part 3 of the unit.
- The **glossary** at the back of the book lists the useful words from each unit with their Cobuild dictionary definitions.
- Two audio **CDs** accompany the book. These contain the listening exercises. When you see this icon ◀)) please play the CD. CD1 features language at a pre-intermediate level speed and CD2 features language that is a little faster. This is to help you prepare for the speed that features in the IELTS test.

Unit structure

Each unit starts with the **Aims** of the unit. They outline the key language and skills covered.

Part 1: Language development provides exercises on vocabulary related to the topic as well as key grammar related to the IELTS Task covered in the unit. Clear structures are provided.

Part 2: Skills development provides step-by-step exercises and guidance on specific question types that appear in the test. There are explanations and examples that show you how to approach each question type. Useful tips are highlighted to help you develop successful test-taking strategies.

Part 3: Exam practice provides one exam practice question for either Task 1 or Task 2 in a format that follows the actual exam. You can use this to check whether or not you are ready for the test.

Finally, a **checklist** summarises the key points covered in the unit.

Other features

Exam information boxes in each unit provide key background information about the IELTS Listening exam.

Exam tip boxes provide essential exam techniques and strategies.

Watch out! boxes highlight common errors in the exam.

Study tips

- Each unit contains approximately three hours of study material.
- Try to answer the questions without looking at a dictionary to develop the skill of guessing the meaning of unknown words from context. This is important because dictionaries cannot be used during the actual exam.
- Use a pencil to complete the exercises, so that you can erase your first answers and do the exercises again for revision.
- Try to revise what you have learnt in Parts 1 and 2 before doing the practice IELTS questions in Part 3. This will improve the quality of your answers, and using the new language will help you to remember it.
- It's recommended that you try and complete all questions in the unit as the skills needed to do well at the IELTS test can only be improved through extensive practice.
- Part 3 contains exam practice questions. You should try and complete Part 3 questions listening to the audio only once, as this gives you the opportunity to practise under exam conditions. Do not look at the audio script at the back of the book while doing Part 3 questions. After you have finished listening, make sure the format and spelling of your answers is correct. Then, check your answers using the answer key.
- Read the answer key carefully as this provides information on what kind of answer is awarded high marks.
- Reading the audio script at the back of the book at the same time as listening to the recording will help you to develop your listening skills and identify answers. Remember that the answers are underlined in the audio scripts.

Other titles

Also available in the *Collins Get Ready for IELTS* series: *Reading*, *Writing* and *Speaking*.

The International English Language Testing System (IELTS) Test

IELTS is jointly managed by the British Council, Cambridge ESOL Examinations and IDP Education, Australia.

There are two versions of the test:

- Academic
- General Training

Academic is for students wishing to study at undergraduate or postgraduate levels in an English-medium environment.

General Training is for people who wish to migrate to an English-speaking country.

This book is primarily for students taking the Academic version.

The Test

There are four modules:

Listening	30 minutes, plus 10 minutes for transferring answers to the answer sheet NB: the audio is heard *only once*. Approx. 10 questions per section Section 1: two speakers discuss a social situation Section 2: one speaker talks about a non-academic topic Section 3: up to four speakers discuss an educational project Section 4: one speaker gives a talk of general academic interest
Reading	60 minutes 3 texts, taken from authentic sources, on general, academic topics. They may contain diagrams, charts, etc. 40 questions: may include multiple choice, sentence completion, completing a diagram, graph or chart, choosing headings, yes/no, true/false questions, classification and matching exercises.
Writing	Task 1: 20 minutes: description of a table, chart, graph or diagram (150 words minimum) Task 2: 40 minutes: an essay in response to an argument or problem (250 words minimum)
Speaking	11–14 minutes A three-part face-to-face oral interview with an examiner. The interview is recorded. Part 1: introductions and general questions (4–5 mins) Part 2: individual long turn (3–4 mins) – the candidate is given a task, has one minute to prepare, then talks for 1–2 minutes, with some questions from the examiner. Part 3: two-way discussion (4–5 mins): the examiner asks further questions on the topic from Part 2, and gives the candidate the opportunity to discuss more abstract issues or ideas.
Timetabling	Listening, Reading and Writing must be taken on the same day, and in the order listed above. Speaking can be taken up to 7 days before or after the other modules.
Scoring	Each section is given a band score. The average of the four scores produces the Overall Band Score. You do not pass or fail IELTS; you receive a score.

IELTS and the Common European Framework of Reference

The CEFR shows the level of the learner and is used for many English as a Foreign Language examinations. The table below shows the approximate CEFR level and the equivalent IELTS Overall Band Score:

CEFR description	CEFR code	IELTS Band Score
Proficient user (Advanced)	C2 C1	9 7–8
Independent user (Intermediate – Upper Intermediate)	B2 B1	5–6.5 4–5

This table contains the general descriptors for the band scores 1–9:

IELTS Band Scores		
9	Expert user	Has fully operational command of the language: appropriate, accurate and fluent with complete understanding.
8	Very good user	Has fully operational command of the language, with only occasional unsystematic inaccuracies and inappropriacies. Misunderstandings may occur in unfamiliar situations. Handles complex detailed argumentation well.
7	Good user	Has operational command of the language, though with occasional inaccuracies, inappropriacies and misunderstandings in some situations. Generally handles complex language well and understands detailed reasoning.
6	Competent user	Has generally effective command of the language despite some inaccuracies, inappropriacies and misunderstandings. Can use and understand fairly complex language, particularly in familiar situations.
5	Modest user	Has partial command of the language, coping with overall meaning in most situations, though is likely to make many mistakes. Should be able to handle basic communication in own field.
4	Limited user	Basic competence is limited to familiar situations. Has frequent problems in understanding and expression. Is not able to use complex language.
3	Extremely limited user	Conveys and understands only general meaning in very familiar situations. Frequent breakdowns in communication occur.
2	Intermittent user	No real communication is possible except for the most basic information using isolated words or short formulae in familiar situations and to meet immediate needs. Has great difficulty understanding spoken and written English.
1	Non user	Essentially has no ability to use the language beyond possibly a few isolated words.
0	Did not attempt the test	No assessable information provided.

Marking

The Listening and Reading papers have 40 items, each worth one mark if correctly answered. Here are some examples of how marks are translated into band scores:

Listening: 16 out of 40 correct answers: band score 5
23 out of 40 correct answers: band score 6
30 out of 40 correct answers: band score 7

Reading 15 out of 40 correct answers: band score 5
23 out of 40 correct answers: band score 6
30 out of 40 correct answers: band score 7

Writing and Speaking are marked according to performance descriptors.
Writing: examiners award a band score for each of four areas with equal weighting:

- Task achievement (Task 1)
- Task response (Task 2)
- Coherence and cohesion
- Lexical resource and grammatical range and accuracy

Speaking: examiners award a band score for each of four areas with equal weighting:

- Fluency and coherence
- Lexical resource
- Grammatical range
- Accuracy and pronunciation

For full details of how the examination is scored and marked, go to: www.ielts.org

1 Friends abroad

AIMS: Language related to: travel, timetables, countries, nationalities • Predicting answers
• Recognizing number formats and spellings • Form completion • Note completion
• Multiple-choice questions

Part 1: Vocabulary

Nations and nationalities

1 Quiz: Can you match these countries to the names in the box?

> Egypt   Malaysia   Portugal   Japan   United Arab Emirates (UAE)

a Japan   b Egypt   c Malaysia
d united Arab Emirates   e Portugal

Nationalities are often formed by changing the endings of the names of countries.
Look at the examples in the table below.

Country	+ ending	Nationality
Australia	__ n	Australian
Egypt	__ ian	Egyptian
Britain	__ ish	British
Japan	__ ese	Japanese
Pakistan	__ i	Pakistani

2 Complete the following sentences about national airlines with the correct nationality.

1 Japan Airlines is a ...*Japanese*... airline.
2 Air China is a ...*Chinese*... airline.
3 Egyptair is an ...*Egyptian*... airline.
4 Emirates is an ...*Emirati*... airline.
5 TAP Portugal is a ...*Portuguese*... airline.
6 Malaysia Airlines is a ...*Malaysian*... airline.

3 Complete these notes with information from the flight arrivals board below.

Spanish flight arrived at (1) ...*5 o'clock*... *4.50*
Flight CCA1550 from (2) ...*Beijing*... arrived at 6.00.
Emirati flight no (3) ...*UAE 1880*... delayed.
Flight TAP1330 due 7.30 from (4) ...*Lisbon*... landed Terminal (5) ...*16*...

Flight Arrivals					
Time due	From	Airline	Flight	Terminal	Status
05.00	Madrid	Iberia	IBE0567	50	Arrived 04.50
06.15	Beijing	Air China	CCA1550	15	Arrived 06.00
06.50	Dubai	Emirates	UAE1880	13	Delayed
07.30	Lisbon	TAP	TAP1330	16	Landed

4 Now listen to a taxi driver talking to a travel agent about the flight arrivals and check your answers.

01

Exam information | Section one

In Section One of the Listening test you will hear two people talking in an everyday or social situation. You may have to complete notes or a form with details of names, addresses, times or dates. You will need to listen carefully for spellings and numbers.

Exam tip

Before you listen, look at the information you have been given to complete. Predicting the kind of answers you need will help you to focus on what you are going to hear.

🔊 **1**
02

You will hear a conversation between two friends planning a visit. Predict the kind of information you will have to listen for (numbers, letters, time, name, etc.). Then listen and complete the notes

Sam arrives at (1) *6:50 pm* on: (2) *Wednesday 6th July*
Airline/Flight number: (3) *BA 30 25*

Watch Out!

It's easy to confuse certain numbers that sound similar, for example: fif<u>teen</u> and <u>fif</u>ty. Listen very carefully to hear which part of the word is spoken with more emphasis.

🔊 **2**
03

Listen and circle the numbers you hear. Then match them with their written forms.

(18)   (13)   (15)   30   (80)   (40)   14   50

fifteen   thirteen   eighteen   fourteen   fifty   forty   eighty   thirty

🔊 **3**
04

Now listen to these sentences and write down the numbers you hear.

(1) *14*   (2) *40*   (3) *50*   4 *16.15*   5 *17.30*

🔊 **4**
05-06

Listen to the following conversations and choose the correct letter a, b or c.

i a McKeon   (b) McEwan   c MacKeon

ii a Westborne   b Westerborne   (c) Westbourne

🔊 **5**
07

You will hear a telephone conversation in which Sam is booking a taxi. First look at the form below and think about the kind of information you will need. Then listen and complete the form.

Exam tip

You will be expected to know the spellings of common words and names. Any usual names will be spelt out for you. An answer spelt wrongly will be marked incorrect, so get plenty of practice before the exam.

PLEASE USE BLOCK CAPITALS

NAME OF PASSENGER:	SAM WILLIAMS
PICK-UP DATE AND TIME:	Wed 6th July 7:20 am (1) 3:20 am
PICK-UP POINT: NO. & STREET: TOWN: POSTCODE:	(2) 60 WILLOWSIDE BANK (3) ABINGDON (4) OX14 3HB
MOBILE NUMBER:	(5) 07789 612744
DESTINATION:	HEATHROW – TERMINAL 5

🔊 **6**
08

You will hear a conversation between a flight attendant and a passenger completing a landing card before arriving in the UK. Complete the form.

LANDING CARD Immigration Act 1971	Please complete clearly in English and BLOCK CAPITALS

Family name

LIU

First name(s)

HUA FANG
(1) Hua Fang

Sex

☐ M   ☒ F

Date of birth

(2) | D | D | M | M | Y | Y | Y | Y |
    | 1 | 7 | 1 | 2 | 1 | 9 | 9 | 4 |

Town and country of birth

SHENZHEN   CHINA

Nationality

CHINESE

Occupation

STUDENT

Contact address in the UK (in full)

(3) 13 Park Road Brighton
BN40 4GR

Exam tip

When you complete a form, it is important to keep to the required number of words for each answer. You will be told how many words to use, e.g. NO MORE THAN TWO WORDS AND/OR A NUMBER. If you write too many words, your answer will be marked incorrect.

A hyphenated word counts as one word, e.g. *mother-in-law*. A number can be written in letters or numbers, e.g. *twelve* or *12*; either way, it counts as one word.

Section 1

🔊
09

Questions 1–7

You will hear a telephone conversation between a hotel receptionist and a caller making a reservation. Complete the form below. Write **NO MORE THAN THREE WORDS AND/OR A NUMBER** for each answer.

Silver Tulip Hotel	
Number of nights	*1*
Type of room: *(circle one)*	(1) Single / Double – twin beds / Double – king-sized bed
Name	(2) Edward Francis
Home address	(3) 23 Cypriess Avenue, Cambridge
Postcode	(4) CB3 9NF
Transport	(5) Taxi
Meals	(6) Breakfast
Date of arrival	(7) Friday, 16th April

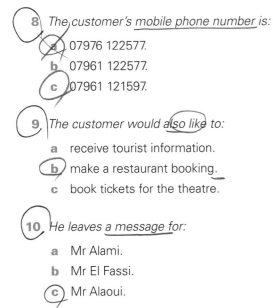

🔊
10

Questions 8–10

Listen to the next part of the conversation and choose the correct letter, *a*, *b* or *c*.

8 The customer's <u>mobile phone number</u> is:

  a 07976 122577.

  b 07961 122577.

  c 07961 121597.

9 The customer would also like to:

  a receive tourist information.

  b make a restaurant booking.

  c book tickets for the theatre.

10 He leaves a <u>message</u> for:

  a Mr Alami.

  b Mr El Fassi.

  c Mr Alaoui.

Exam tip

During the exam, listen very carefully and don't presume the first information you hear is always correct. Sometimes the speaker can change his/her mind and correct the information given.

Now listen again to check your answers before you look at the answer key.

Progress check

How many boxes can you tick? You should work towards being able to tick them all.

Did you …
listen closely for numbers that sound similar? ☐
check your spellings? ☐
check that you have written the correct number of words in the answers? ☐

2 Food and cooking

Part 1: Vocabulary

Types of food

meat

dairy products

vegetables

fruit

1 Complete the table by putting the following foods into the correct column.

potatoes   bananas   cabbage   turkey   lamb   pineapple
cheese   butter   carrots   beef   cherries   yoghurt

meat	dairy products	vegetables	fruit
turkey	cheese	potatoes	bananas
lamb	butter	cabbage	pineapple
beef	yogurt	carrots	cherries

Countable and Uncountable Nouns

Some nouns can be countable <u>and</u> uncountable. They often become uncountable when they are prepared for eating, e.g.

There are ten chickens in the field. / Would you like some chicken?
I bought two cauliflowers yesterday. / My son doesn't like cauliflower.

2 Say whether the following foods are C (countable) or U (uncountable) or C/U (both countable and uncountable).

1 carrot ...C/U...
2 rice ...U...
3 lamb ...C/U...
4 bean ...C/U...
5 butter ...U...

6 onion ...C/U...
7 bread ...U...
8 egg ...C/U...
9 pea ...C/U...
10 coffee ...C/U...

Cooking methods

3   Write the correct letter (A–E) next to each method of cooking.

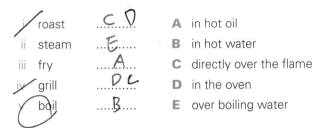

i	roast	..C..	**A** in hot oil
ii	steam	..E..	**B** in hot water
iii	fry	..A..	**C** directly over the flame
iv	grill	..D C..	**D** in the oven
v	boil	..B..	**E** over boiling water

Weights and measures

4   Choose from the following list of weights and measures to complete the list of ingredients for making pancakes.

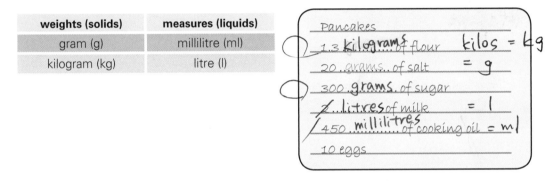

weights (solids)	measures (liquids)
gram (g)	millilitre (ml)
kilogram (kg)	litre (l)

Pancakes

1.3 kilograms of flour   kilos = kg

20 grams of salt   = g

300 grams of sugar

2 litres of milk   = l

450 millilitres of cooking oil = ml

10 eggs

Exam tip

In some tasks in the IELTS exam, the information that you read in the question will be expressed in different words in the audio. So you will need to listen out for synonyms and paraphrasing. You will be able to practise this skill throughout this book.

---

5   Complete these equivalents.

¼ = a quarter   ½ = a half   (1) $\frac{3}{4}$ = three quarters   ⅓ = a third

⅔ = (2) two thirds   ⅛ = one eighth   ⅝ = (3) five eighths

(4) ⅞ = seven eighths

◀)) **6**   You will hear a list of ingredients. Circle the correct quantity. Then write a different way to
11   express the same quantity.

1	apples	1 kilo / ½ kilo	500 g
2	sugar	250 g / 215 g	½ kilo
3	flour	330 g / 130 g	⅓ kilo
4	butter	120 g / 200 g	⅕ kilo
5	milk	⅕ l / 5 l	200 ml

Exam information | Section two

In Section Two of the Listening test you will hear one person talking about a topic of general interest. You may have to complete notes, a table or a flow chart describing a process.

🔊 **1**
12

You will hear a chef giving her students a list of ingredients for a regional dish. Match the ingredients with the quantities. You will not use all the quantities. Before you begin, read through the answer options and think of different ways to express the same quantities.

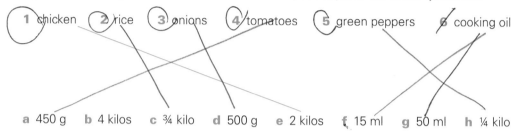

1 chicken   2 rice   3 onions   4 tomatoes   5 green peppers   6 cooking oil

a 450 g   b 4 kilos   c ¾ kilo   d 500 g   e 2 kilos   f 15 ml   g 50 ml   h ¼ kilo

2

You are going to hear an explanation of how to cook pancakes, or crêpes. Tick the boxes below for the kind of information you expect to hear.

time of day ☐	spelling ☐	date ☐	weights ✓
ingredients ✓	instructions ✓	colours ☐	address ☐

Exam tip

When you have to complete notes about the stages in a process, for example to complete a flow chart, it will help you to listen carefully for words that indicate the order of the different parts of the procedure, such as *first, then, after that* and *at the end*.

🔊 **3**
13

Listen to the recording and put the photos in the correct order.

...D.....   ...E....   ...A.....   ...G.....   ...F.....   ...C.....   ...B.....

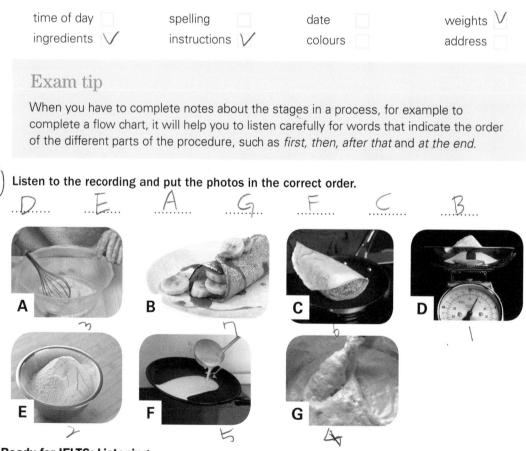

A   B   C   D

E   F   G

Exam tip

When you are asked to do a completion task, you may be told to use words from the recording. If this is the case, you may have to omit unimportant words, like *a* or *the* to keep to the word count.

🔊 **4**
14

Now you will hear someone describing how to cook a traditional dessert. Before you listen, read and think about which words <u>might</u> go in the gaps.

Then listen and complete the flow chart. Write NO MORE THAN FOUR WORDS for each answer.

cut the apples

Peel and (1) cut apples in slices	→	Cook (2) with sugar	→	Mix (3) blackberries and apples
Add (the) (6) sugar	←	Rub (5) flour and butter (together)	←	Put in bottom of (4) ~~dishes~~ (a) baking dish
Put mixture (7) crumble on top = on top of fruit	→	Bake for (8) 30 minutes	→	

🔊 **5**
15

You will hear a student representative welcoming new students to the university and explaining a little about traditional English meals. First read the notes below.

Then listen and complete them. Write NO MORE THAN TWO WORDS OR A NUMBER for each answer.

Very popular dish : Fish and chips: fried in (1) deep fat ~~pots~~

- not (2) healthy   Popular esp. (3) Friday nights

Another traditional meal: Sunday lunch

(4) Roast   meat, with (5) vegetables

Traditionally eaten (6) at home

Section 2

Questions 1–4

You will hear a talk on nutrition. Complete the notes. Write NO MORE THAN TWO WORDS for each answer.

Topic: Healthy eating
- definition
- reasons why people don't (1) .... *eat properly*
- ideas for (2) .... *improving situations*

Healthy eating is:
- balanced diet
- eating the (3) ..*right*.... *amount*
Note: balanced diet incl. meat, veg, fruit, cereals & (4) ..*dairy foods*...

Exam tip

In some tasks you will be asked to choose several correct answers from a list. Always read the options before you listen to the recording. After listening, you will be able to eliminate the incorrect ones. Make sure you choose the required number of answer options.

Questions 5–7

Listen to the next part of the talk. Choose **THREE** letters a–h. Give three reasons why the speaker thinks so many people have an unhealthy diet.

a It is cheaper to buy packet food.

b People do not know how to eat healthily.

c It is cheaper to buy fast food.

d They prefer fast food.

e They do not like packet food.

f It is quicker to buy fast food.

g They have to plan their meals.

h Schools teach children about a balanced diet.

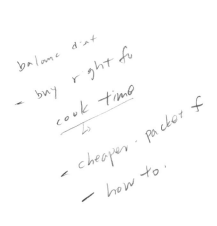

5 ....*f*.... 6 ....*a*.... 7 ....*b*....

Questions 8–10

Listen to the last part of the recording and complete the table. Write NO MORE THAN ONE WORD for each answer.

Group responsible:		
(8) ~~School~~ *Government*	(9) ~~schools~~	(10) *families / Family*
Limit advertising for unhealthy food	Stop selling unhealthy snacks and drinks	Make sure children eat a balanced diet
Educate the public about a healthy diet	Provide children with fresh and healthy options	

Progress check

How many boxes can you tick? You should work towards being able to tick them all.

Did you …

practise listening to different accents?

read through all the questions before you listened to the recording and think about words you expected to hear?

think about words to describe different stages in a process (first, second, then, next …) when you have to complete a flow chart?

make sure you used the correct number of words in your answers?

3 Presentations

AIMS: Language related to: presentations and academic subjects • Identifying future plans and stages in a presentation • Keeping to word count • Completing sentences and tables • Labelling diagrams • Multiple-choice questions

Part 1: Vocabulary

Presentations

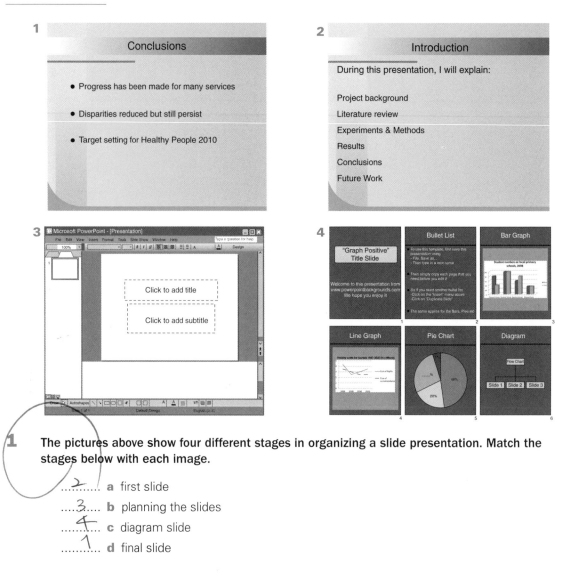

1 The pictures above show four different stages in organizing a slide presentation. Match the stages below with each image.

........2...... **a** first slide

......3.... **b** planning the slides

........4.... **c** diagram slide

..........1.... **d** final slide

2 Listen to these words and underline the part that is stressed in each one. The first one has been done for you.

19

1 intro<u>duce</u>   intro<u>duc</u>tion
2 presen<u>tation</u>   pre<u>sent</u> (v)   <u>pre</u>sent (n)
3 sug<u>gest</u>   sug<u>ges</u>tion
4 pro<u>ject</u> (v)   pro<u>ject</u> (n)   pro<u>jec</u>tor
5 in<u>form</u>   infor<u>ma</u>tion
6 ex<u>plain</u>   expla<u>na</u>tion

3 Now listen to this short conversation and underline the word you hear in each pair. You will hear them in the same order.

20

introduce / introduction

suggest / suggestion

✓ *present (v) / present (n)*

project (v) / project (n)

inform / information

explain / explanation

Vocabulary groups

4 It is useful to sort words into vocabulary groups when they refer to the same kind of information, e.g. *female – woman – lady – mother*.

Write the words that have a similar meaning in the boxes below.

plan   image   badpoints   graph   French   Arabic
Chinese   cons   chart   Italian   benefits   table
dangers   pros   painting   good points   photograph

diagram: plan   graph   chart   table

picture: image   painting   photograph

language: French   Arabic   chinese   Italian

advantages: cons pros   benefits   good points

disadvantages: badpoints   dangers   pros
                                             cons

Exam information | Section three

In Section Three of the Listening test you will hear a group of people talking about a topic related to education or training. You will be asked to do different tasks in this section, and some of these will require you to identify the ideas and opinions of the individual speakers.

Exam tip

In this type of question, where there are several speakers, it is useful to identify them as early as possible. Listen carefully and write their names on the exam paper, leaving enough room to make a note of any opinions too.

🔊 **1** **You will hear a group of students talking about a project they are planning to present. Choose the correct letter, *a*, *b* or *c*.**
21

  i   *Italian painting is*
      a the subject
      b the topic
      c course

  ii *Who originally wants to discuss one painter?*
      a Edward
      b Farouk
      c Mandy

  iii *Mandy suggests*   single
      a Michelangelo and Botticelli.
      b Michelangelo.
      c Michelangelo and Leonardo da Vinci.

  iv *Beth suggests Botticelli because*
      a everyone else will choose him.
      b his style of painting is different.
      c he's a great artist.

Exam tip

With multiple-choice questions, remember to read all the options before you choose the answer. Some of the answers may look similar and you should check the details before you decide.

🔊 **2**
22
Now you will hear the students planning the slides they are going to prepare for their group presentation. Complete the notes below. Write NO MORE THAN TWO WORDS OR A NUMBER for each answer.

[handwritten: a comparison]

Intro: Michelangelo and Botticelli: (1) .... *[handwritten: comparison, title]*

Total no. of slides: (2) .... *[handwritten: 8 & 6]*

Intro

2 slides each Michelangelo and Botticelli

2 slides: How Michelangelo and Botticelli are (3) *[handwritten: similar]* and how they are (4) *[handwritten: different]*

Conclusion

🔊 **3**
23
Listen to two of the students discussing the best way to design a slide and label the drawing below. Write NO MORE THAN TWO WORDS for each answer.

(1) *[handwritten: title box]*

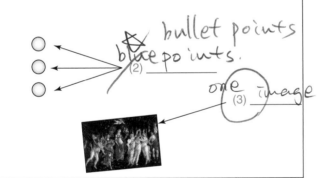

(2) *[handwritten: bullet points / blue points]*

(3) *[handwritten: one image]*

Exam tip

Remember to read all the answers carefully before you listen to the recording. When you have to choose more than one correct answer, it may help you to cross out the wrong answers as you listen.

🔊 **4**
24
Listen to the four students discussing their presentation and underline the TWO correct answers.

What do the students have to *decide*?

a   whether or not to put the slides about Botticelli before Michelangelo

b   which artist is most famous

c   which artist Beth will talk about

d   where to put Farouk's slides

e   whether to talk about Michelangelo first

[handwritten: B, B, M]

Section 3

🔊
25

Questions 1–4

Listen to the recording of three students talking to their tutor about the presentation they are planning. Choose the correct letter, *a*, *b* or *c*.

i The topic of the presentation is

   a how mobile phones are designed. ✓

   b the risks caused by mobile phones.

   c how mobile phones are used. ✓

ii The introduction explains the

   a dangers of mobile phones.

   b importance of mobile phones.

   c importance of understanding the dangers of mobile phones.

iii On the second slide, the students are planning to

   a explain why mobile phones are dangerous.

   b point out some different kinds of risks.

   c mention ways to avoid the risks.

iv The tutor suggests

   a not discussing the dangers of mobile phones.

   b discussing the benefits of mobile phones.

   c having an argument.

🔊
26

Questions 5–7

Listen to the next part of the recording and complete the slides. Write ONE WORD ONLY.

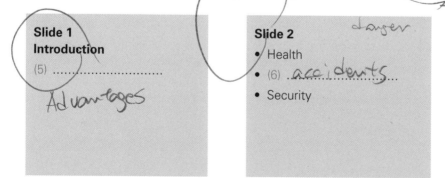

Slide 1
Introduction

(5) ....

Advantages

Slide 2

danger

• Health

• (6) *accidents*

• Security

Slide 3

(7) ....*suggestions*........ for avoiding dangers

🔊 27

Questions 8–10

Listen to the last part of the recording and complete the sentences. Write NO MORE THAN TWO WORDS OR A NUMBER.

8 The actual talk will last for ....*1 minutes*.... *10 min.*

9 Each student will speak for ....*2 minutes*....

10 The slides must all have the .... *same style.*

Progress check

How many boxes can you tick? You should work towards being able to tick them all.

Did you …

read all the questions before you listened to the recording? ☐

think about other words on the topic that you expect to hear? ☐

write the names of the speakers, ready to make a note of their ideas? ☐

look carefully at the multiple-choice options that look similar so you can listen for the correct details? ☐

Review 1

1 Pronunciation: Most of the letters of the alphabet are pronounced with the following set of sounds:

sound	example
/ei/	A
/iː/	E
/e/	F
/ai/	I
/iuː/	U

Note: O /əʊ/ and R /ɑː/ do not share a sound with any other letter.

28 Listen. Pause the recording after each letter and write the letter in the correct column.

/ei/	/iː/	/e/	/ai/	/iuː/	O	R
A	E	F	I	U	O	R
H	B	L	~~X~~	Q		
J	C	M	Y	W		
K	D	N				
	G	S				
	P	X				
	T	Z				
	V					

2 Word formation: Complete the passage with the correct form of the words in brackets:

(1) .....British..... (Britain) Airways apologizes for the late (2) ...departure... (depart) of (3) ...flight... (fly) BA421. This is due to the late (4) ...arrive arrival... (arrive) of the aircraft from New York. Please go to the airline (5) ...information... (inform) desk if you have to make a (6) ...connection... (connect) to reach your final destination.

3 Put the following words into the plural form, where possible. If the word is uncountable, write *U*. There may be two possibilities for some words.

ex) mashed potato

1 onion ...onions...
2 flour ...U...
3 potato ...potatoes...
4 milk ...U...

5 bean ...U beans...
6 cherry ...cherries...
7 coffee ...U...
8 chicken ...chickens... U chicken & food

4 Circle the word that does not belong in each list. What do the others have in common?

1 first, third, fourth, one .... one .... *ordinal numbers*
2 ingredient, gram, ounce, kilo ...... *ingredient* ...... *units of weight*
3 dinner, dish, lunch, breakfast ...... *dish* ...... *meals*
4 after, who, then, next ...... *who* ...... *sequence linking words*
5 area, section, zone, door ...... *door* ...... *synonyms*
6 wi-fi, restaurant, snack bar, café ...... *wi-fi* ...... *places to eat*
7 tea, milk, juice, beans ...... *beans* ...... *drinks*
8 roast, boil, pan, fry ...... *pan* ...... *cooking methods*
9 carrot, cauliflower, onion, banana ...... *banana* ...... *vegetables*
10 milk, cheese, egg, cream ...... *cream* ...... *dairy products*
egg

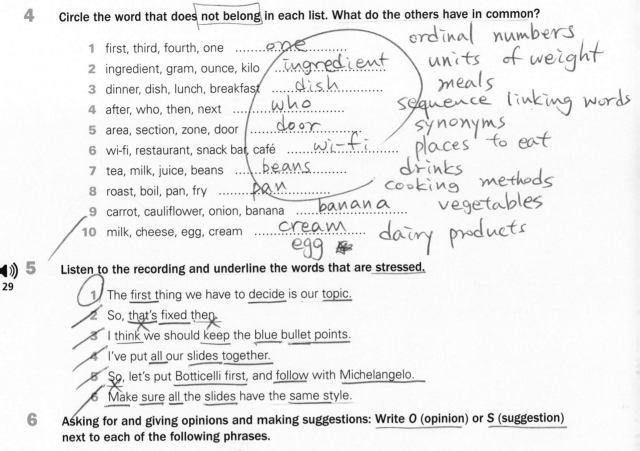

5 Listen to the recording and underline the words that are stressed.

29

1 The first thing we have to decide is our topic.
2 So, that's fixed then.
3 I think we should keep the blue bullet points.
4 I've put all our slides together.
5 So, let's put Botticelli first, and follow with Michelangelo.
6 Make sure all the slides have the same style.

6 Asking for and giving opinions and making suggestions: Write *O* (opinion) or *S* (suggestion) next to each of the following phrases.

1 What do you think? ...... O ......
2 Let's ... . S ......
3 Do you agree? ...... O ......
4 I think... ...... O ......
5 Don't you think ...? ...... O ......
6 Why don't we ... . S ......
7 How about ... . S ......
8 You could ... . S ......
9 What about ...? ...... S ......
10 I don't think ... . O ......

4 Work

AIMS: Language related to: work and the workplace • Listening for main ideas • Listening for detailed information • Distinguishing fact from opinion • Completing notes • Short-answer questions • Matching information

Part 1: Vocabulary

People at work

1 The pictures above show people at work. Match each picture with the person's occupation. Write the letter.

   1 farmer .*B*...   **2** police officer .*D*...   **3** businessman ..*A*...   **4** doctor ...*C*...

2 Complete these definitions with one of the occupations in the pictures.

   1 A .*businessman*. is a person who makes money by selling goods or services.
   2 A .*police officer*. protects the public from criminals.
   3 A .*doctor*.. is a person who is qualified in medicine.
   4 A person who grows food is called a .*farmer*.

Extending vocabulary

In the Listening test, the words on the answer sheet may not always be the same as the ones you hear on the recording. So, it is important to know as many words as possible that have similar meanings or are connected with the topic of the recording.

3 Complete the word map on the next page with verbs from the list.

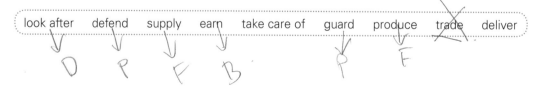

look after   defend   supply   earn   take care of   guard   produce   trade   deliver

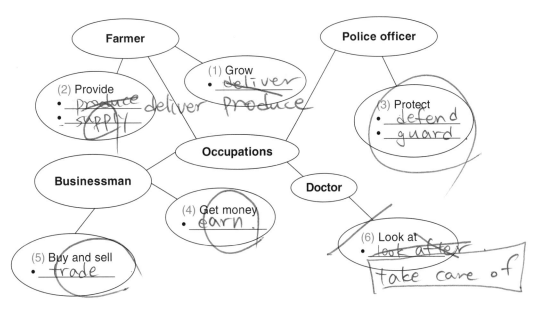

Words that go together

Some words change their meaning when they are combined with other words, for example, verbs combined with different prepositions form different phrasal verbs.

4 **Complete the table with the appropriate preposition.**

Verb	Preposition	Meaning
1 look	*for*	*search*
2 look	after	care for
3 look	at	examine
4 look	over	check
5 look	through	scan

5 **Complete the following sentences with the most suitable phrasal verb from the table in Exercise 4.**

1 The class sometimes *looks through* the newspaper for information about their local town.

2 The family called the police to help them *look for* their son, who was lost.

3 The student asked his tutor to *look over* his essay for mistakes.

4 When they arrived at the hospital, the doctor *looked at* his broken arm.

5 The parents asked the baby-sitter to *look after* their children while they went out.

Exam information | Section four

In Section Four of the Listening test you will hear one person talking about an academic topic of general interest. You may have to complete a summary or notes or give short answers to questions.

Exam tip

Before you listen to each part of the lecture in Section Four read the questions carefully and underline the key words. This will give you some information about the topic in advance and help you focus on the main ideas while you are listening.

A speaker will often introduce the topic of a lecture with a phrase like:

Today I'm going to talk about …

My topic today is …

My lecture this evening will be about …

In today's lecture I'll be talking about …

This week's talk will cover …

I'm here to tell you about …

open

🔊 **1** **Listen to the following introductions and write the topic of each talk.**
30

1 ~~Student's~~ Student's societies

2 working in ~~working in~~ large corporation

3 Working outdoors

4 employment opportunities in institutions of further education

5 job satisfaction

6 Five jobs / finding a job / adding of

2 **Find two words or phrases in the list below that have a similar meaning to each of the lecture topics in Exercise 1.**

~~in the open air~~   ~~enjoyment~~   ~~employment~~   ~~associations~~   business   ~~outside~~
~~colleges~~   ~~fulfilment~~   ~~universities~~   company   (occupation)   ~~clubs~~   (work)

1 clubs .... associations

2 company .... business

3 in the open air ...... outside

4 colleges .... universities

5 enjoyment .... fulfilment

6 work .... occupation
   employment   work

🔊 **3** Listen to the introductions again. They are slightly different this time. Complete the notes
31 about each topic. Write ONE word only.

1 ~~clubs~~ you can join at university
2 working in a small ~~company~~
3 jobs that involve spending a lot of time ~~outside~~
4 employment in ~~universities~~
5 job ~~for filling~~ ~~fulfilment~~
6 how to find ~~employment~~

Exam tip

When you have identified the key words / main ideas in the questions, listen carefully
for more detailed information. While you listen, use any headings on the question
sheet to guide you, and pay close attention to the key words.

In some questions you will have to decide whether the speaker is giving factual information or
expressing their opinion. Speakers may use phrases like *I enjoy* or *I like* to show their feelings
or they may use more formal expressions to introduce opinions, for example: *It seems to me;
My impression is …*

🔊 **4** You will hear an extract from two interviews with people about their work. Complete the
32-33 notes. Write no more than TWO WORDS for each answer.

Alice works on (a) ~~a farm~~
– grows (2) ~~fruit~~
– keeps (3) ~~chickens~~ ducks and cows
– worst part of job – going out in winter to
  feed (4) ~~dark~~ ~~animals~~
– likes working outdoors in the (5) ~~summer~~
– trucks deliver to (6) ~~load supermarkets~~
– supplies (7) ~~supermarket~~ with milk,
  eggs, cheese ~~local shops~~
– sells directly to (8) ~~people~~ in farm shop

Wei Long works as a (9) ~~businessman~~ ~~technology~~
– graduated in (10) ~~Information~~
– ambition – earn living through (11) ~~experience~~ ~~trade~~
– has own (12) ~~small company~~
– sells (13) ~~computer parts~~
– (14) ~~receptionist~~ looks after the office
– likes making own (15) ~~boss decisions~~
– wouldn't like to work in a (16) ~~big company~~

◀)) **5**
34

You will hear Khalidah talking about the patients, doctors and nurses in the Accident and Emergency Unit. Write a letter a–f next to each group of people. You will not use all the options.

What does Khalidah say about each group of people?

a   see the patients after they have talked to the nurse
b   have had accidents in the work place
c   discover what is wrong with the patients
d   look after patients who are out of danger
e   arrange for patients to go home in an ambulance
f   have had accidents in cars or at home

1   patients   ....
2   doctors   a e c
3   nurses   d

Part 3: Exam practice

Section 4

Questions 1–4

35

You will hear a woman talking to some students about her job. Complete the notes with words from the recording. Write NO MORE THAN TWO WORDS for each answer.

Job: (1) ...police... officer... for five years
Studied: (2) ...law... at university
Interested in (3) ...pratical... side, not theory
Accepted for (4) ...training... after graduating

(handwritten notes: police o / law ann order. / pratical / train)

Questions 5–7

36

Now you will hear the next part of the talk. Answer the question. Choose THREE answers from a–f.

What does the speaker think are the disadvantages of police work?

a danger of being attacked
b protecting the public
c not being available for family celebrations
d special training in avoiding trouble
e working difficult hours
f working with the public

(handwritten: working hours / celebra / prevent danger arrest)

5 ...c e... 6 ...d c... 7 ...a...

Questions 8–10

37

Listen to the last part of the recording and answer the questions. Write no more than TWO WORDS.

8 What does the speaker think about the financial rewards of police work? ...well-paid...
9 What kind of people do the police sometimes have to protect? ...celebrities...
10 What does the speaker want to be in the future? ...Detective...

(handwritten: job satisfaction)

Progress check

How many boxes can you tick? You should work towards being able to tick them all.

Did you …
underline the key words in the questions?
think about other words with the same meaning as the key words?
read all the possible answers before you listened to the recording?
check that you have not used more words than you are asked to?

5 On campus services

Part 1: Vocabulary

Campus services

1 .... 2 .... 3 .... 4 ....

1 The pictures above show buildings on a university campus. Label the buildings with the words in the box.

> halls of residence   library   medical centre   sports centre

2 Now match the buildings with the definitions below. You will not use all the definitions.

   1 This is where you go to get fit. ....

   2 You go here when you are sick and need to get a prescription. ....

   3 This is where you will find all kinds of reference materials, including journals, films, computers and all the information you need for your studies. ....

   4 This is where students live on campus. ....

   5 You go here when you want to listen to music. ....

Spelling

> ### Watch Out!
> Some words sound the same, but are spelt differently. In the Listening test, you must spell your answers correctly, or you will lose points.

3 Choose the correct spelling to complete the sentences.

1 The lecturer told his students to read .... the article quickly. (*threw / through / though*)

2 .... was a long queue of people waiting at the medical centre to see the doctor. (*Their / They're / There*)

3 The university has a number of .... (*restuarants / restaurants / resteurents*)

4 A lot of people enjoy meeting visitors from .... countries. (*foriegn / foreing / foreign*)

5 To get to the library, take the first road on the left and keep walking .... you get to the end of the road. (*untill / until / unntil*)

6 The tutor's office is on the .... floor. (*twelvth / twefth / twelfth*).

Prepositions

Exam information | Labelling plans

In the exam you may have to identify buildings by their location on a plan, and you will need to recognize the prepositions that indicate where things are.

4 Sometimes there is more than one word to describe the same position, for example: *beside, by, next to.* In each group of words, circle the preposition or phrase that does NOT belong to the group.

1 on top of, into, over, above

2 next to, far away, nearby, close to

3 outside, inside, within, into

4 behind, opposite, in front of, facing

5 beside, next to, between, at the side of

5 Read the description of a university campus and label the buildings on the plan.

The library is in the middle of the campus. It's next to the theatre. There's a shop behind the library, between the bank and the bookshop. The Student Union building is opposite the theatre, beside the round building, which is the night club. The Sports Centre is on the other side of the green, facing the Medical Centre.

A Sports Centre   B Night Club   C Student Union   D Shop   E Theatre

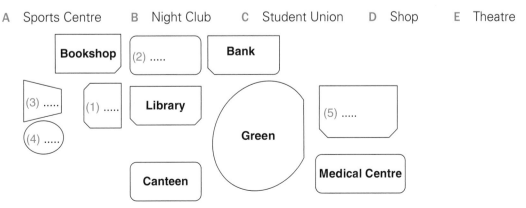

Exam information | Sentence completion

In the exam you may have to complete some sentences. You will use the exact words you hear in the recording, but it is important to make sure your answers are grammatically correct. You will lose points if they are not.

1   Complete the sentences with the correct ending from the box.

> the corner   the right   to the lake   straight ahead of you   opposite   Medical Centre

   1   Take the lift up to the twelfth floor and the tutor's office is the third door on ....

   2   To get to the bank, cross the road at the library and turn left at ....

   3   Go down the footpath to the main road and the station's right ....

   4   Turn left at the top of the stairs, go along to the end of the corridor and you'll see the seminar room ....

   5   Take the second road on the right, then, first left and you'll find the physics building next to the ....

   6   Go along the main path as far as the canteen, then follow it round to the left until you get ....

◀)) 2   You will hear six short conversations, where one person is explaining to another how to find
38   different places on campus. Before you listen, make a note of some of the expressions you expect to hear. Complete the sentences as you listen. Pay attention to your spelling and grammar, and write **NO MORE THAN THREE WORDS**.

   1   The Sports Centre is on the other side ....

   2   The lecture theatre in the Law School is on ....

   3   To reach the Business School, you take the footpath ....

   4   The theatre is ....

   5   The nearest bus stop is opposite the ....

   6   The bank is .... to the shop.

Exam information | Short-answer questions

In another type of question you may be asked to give short answers to the questions. You will hear the words you should use on the recording. You do not need to change them. But it is very important to pay attention to the number of words you write. You will be told how many words to use. This is usually no more than three words and /or a number. Your answer will be marked incorrect if you use too many words.

🔊 **3**
39

Listen to Sandra and Tom talking about the facilities on campus and answer the questions. Write NO MORE THAN TWO WORDS.

1 Which floor is the library coffee shop on? ....

2 What does Sandra like to do there? ....

3 Where is the silent zone? ....

4 Where does Tom live? ....

5 How many people live in Sandra's house? ....

6 What does Tom often do near Sandra's house? ....

Exam tip

In some questions you may be asked to label a map or a plan. You will always hear the information in the same order as the numbered questions. Before you listen, look at the plan on the question paper and pay attention to the information you have been given. This will help you to focus on the context and predict what you may hear.

🔊 **4**
40

Listen to two students talking about the different food outlets on a university campus and label the plan below.

A Fast food hall

B Snack bar

C Mexican restaurant

D College dining room

E Italian restaurant

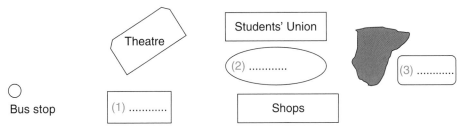

Section 1

Questions 1–4

41

You will hear Lily explaining to Chen how to use the library. Label the plan of the library.

A PC Zone
B Library Café
C Cookbooks
D Travel
E Silent zone

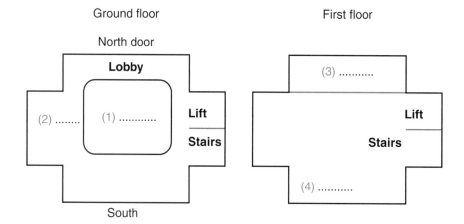

Ground floor   First floor

North door

Lobby

(3) ....

(2) .... (1) .... **Lift**   **Lift**

Stairs   **Stairs**

(4) ....

South

Questions 5–7

42

Listen to the next part of the recording and complete the sentences. Write only TWO WORDS.

5 First look up the title in the ....

6 The class mark is one or two letters and ....

7 The .... shows you where to look for the books.

🔊
43

Questions 8–10

Listen to the last part of the recording and answer the questions. WRITE NO MORE THAN THREE WORDS.

    8 What do you need to scan first? ....

    9 What does the scanner do when you scan a book? ....

  10 What does the system do at the end? ....

Progress check

How many boxes can you tick? You should work towards being able to tick them all.

Did you …

think about the words you expected to hear before you listened? ☐

look carefully at the information you have on the question paper? ☐

listen for key words by concentrating on the words that are spoken with more stress? ☐

make sure your answers were grammatically correct when you completed the sentences? ☐

6 Staying safe

AIMS: Language related to: crime and protection • Listening for key words and synonyms • Recognizing categories • Word formation • Multiple-choice questions • Short-answer questions • Completing tables

Part 1: Vocabulary

Crime

1 The following words are all connected with crime and staying safe. Tick the ones you can see in the pictures.

break into ☐   thief ☐   knife ☐   gun ☐   gang ☐   pickpocket ☐

2 Now write the words in correct columns in the table.

crime   knife   gun   gang   dangerous   careful
steal   rob   break into   thief   attack   safe

Noun	Verb	Adjective

Words with similar meanings

> **Exam tip**
>
> As you are reading through the questions before starting the Listening test, you will be identifying key words in order to predict what you are going to hear. As you do this, try to think of synonyms for the key words. Paraphrasing is very common in the IELTS Listening test, so it is very important that you practise this skill.

3 Complete the following sentences with words from the box that have the same meaning as the word in brackets. Make sure your answers are grammatically correct.

> steal   safe   robber   shoplifter   gang   pickpocket   burglar

1 A (thief) broke into the office and (took) a laptop.
2 While the friends were at the night club, a (thief) took their wallets out of their jackets.
3 A police officer went to the shop to talk to a (thief) who was taking the goods out of the shop without paying.
4 A (group) of (thieves) broke into a bank and took £1,000,000 over the weekend.
5 The students were advised to keep their passports in a (secure) place when they went on holiday.

Collocations

Some words are often used together. For example: *do + homework*, *make + cake*. In the exam, it will help to know which words go together and what you expect to hear.

4 Match the words that are often used together.

take	the police
watch out	up
call	for
lock	scene
crime	to court

5 Complete the text with phrases from exercise 4. Check that your verb tenses are correct.

When the receptionist arrived at Goodmead Primary school on Monday, she found that someone had (1) .... the office and stolen several laptops, so she (2) .... They came to look at the (3) .... straight away and advised her to make sure she (4) .... the office every evening in future. They also suggested that she should (5) .... any strangers nearby. Two days later, the police called to say that they had caught the thieves and arrested them. They said they would (6) .... them .... in the next few days.

🔊 **6** Listen to the recording and check your answers.
44

Pronunciation

When you listen to people speaking, it is sometimes difficult to hear the end of one word and the beginning of the next. This often happens when:
- the first word ends with the same sound that starts the next word, e.g. *take care*.
- the second word begins with a vowel e.g. *watch out*.

🔊 **7** Listen to this sentence from the recording and underline where the words join together.
45

When the receptionist arrived at Goodmead Primary school on Monday, she found that someone had broken into the office and stolen several laptops, so she called the police.

Exam tip

When you are looking at the key words in the questions before listening, don't forget to include the question words. These will tell you what kind of information you need (e.g. *What type of* ... = category, class).

1 Read the following questions and underline the key words and the question words.

1 What is the most common crime in the UK?
2 What two forms of theft does the policewoman mention?
3 Why are people in more danger when they are abroad?
4 What should people leave in the hotel on holiday?
5 What kind of mobile is popular with thieves?

 2
46

Now listen to the recording and answer the questions. Write NO MORE THAN FOUR WORDS.

1 What is the most common crime in the UK?

....

2 What two forms of theft does the policewoman mention?

....

3 Why are people in more danger when they are abroad?

....

4 What should people leave in the hotel?

....

5 What kind of mobile is popular with thieves?

....

Exam information ǀ Table completion

In one type of question you may have to complete a table with no more than two words or a number. The heading will tell you what kind of information you need to focus on. Before you listen, underline the heading of each column in the table.

 3
47

Listen to a talk about emergency phone numbers in different countries and complete the table.

UK	USA	Australia	Germany	India
999				

4 Read the text about staying safe on campus and answer the question. Tick the correct answer.

Security Officer: Our campus is generally a very safe place for students and staff. Crime is very rare, but when it does occur, it's quite often because someone has not been careful enough. They may not have locked their door or they might have gone out alone at night.

What does the security officer say about crime on campus?

a The campus is always safe.

b Crime does not happen very often.

c Crime never happens when people are careful.

Now look at the answers. Notice that the difference between the correct answer and a wrong answer may depend on one word.

a The campus is always safe. ✗
The officer says the *campus is <u>generally</u> a very safe place*, not that it is <u>always</u> safe.

b Crime does not happen very often. ✓
The officer says crime is *very rare*.

c Crime never happens when people are careful. ✗
The officer says crime *often* happens when *someone has not been careful enough*. This does not mean it <u>never</u> happens when people are careful.

🔊 **5** You will hear a talk about staying safe on campus. Choose *a, b* or *c.*
48

i When can students ask a security officer to walk home with them?

    a in the evening   **b** after dark   **c** late at night

ii What does the security officer say students should do if they want to go home late at night and they feel nervous?

    a They should ring campus security.   **c** They should go home alone.

    b They should study in the library.

iii What does the security officer say about national and on campus emergency numbers?

    a They are both 999.   **c** They are not the same.

    b They are both 3333.

iv Why should students call 3333 in an emergency on campus?

    a 999 does not work.   **c** It is faster.

    b It is confusing.

Section 2

🔊 49

Questions 1–4

You will hear a talk about safety in different regions. Complete the table about crime in two different holiday destinations. Write NO MORE THAN TWO WORDS OR A NUMBER.

Region	Type of Crime
(1)	(2)
(3)	(4)

🔊 50

Questions 5–7

Listen to the next part of the recording and answer the questions. Write NO MORE THAN THREE WORDS.

5 What are tourists advised not to wear in the street?

....

6 Where should tourists not go after dark?

....

7 In some parts of Latin America, where do thieves often take money from tourists?

....

🔊 51

Questions 8–10

Listen to the last part of the recording and choose the correct answer to the questions.

8 *What did the travel advisor think about India?*
   a It was dangerous.
   b It was organized.
   c It was safe.

9 *Why does the speaker recommend going to India with a tour group?*
   a because it is more fun
   b because it is less risky
   c because they don't need cash

10 *What did the tour guide tell the tourists not to do?*

    a   speak their own language

    b   go with people they don't know

    c   be nice and friendly

Progress check

How many boxes can you tick? You should work towards being able to tick them all.

Did you …

underline the key words in the question?

compare the answers that looked similar in the multiple-choice questions?

look at the headings in tables to see what kind of information you need?

think about words that often go together so you could predict what
    you expect to hear on the recording?

Review 2

1 Word families: Organize the words into columns by category.

> business   studied   truck   company   doctor   firm   rescue worker   supply
> farmer   graduated   deliver   shop   nurse university   police officer

Trade	Occupation	Education	Transport
business			

2 Complete the sentences with the correct words from the list.

> in   for   after   at   on   around

1 Ahmed asked his tutor to look .... his essay.
2 A team of rescue workers went out to look .... the lost teenagers.
3 The sales team travels .... the world.
4 As a farmer, he enjoys working .... the land.
5 The nurses in the accident and emergency ward look .... patients who are not .... danger.

3 Underline the correct spelling of the words.

1 accommodation, accomodation, acommodation
2 acident, accident, accidant
3 librery, libary, library
4 oposite, opposite, oppisite
5 business, busines, bisness

6 Wednesday, Wendsday, Wedensday
7 Febuary, Febrary, February
8 nesessary, necesary, necessary
9 relevent, relevant, relavant
10 responsable, responsibal, responsible

4 Complete the following sentences with the correct prepositions. Write ONE WORD ONLY in each space.

1 The green is .... the middle of the campus .... front of the library.

2 Turn left .... the top of the road that runs from the entrance.

3 The student union building is .... the corner of the main road and the entrance to the campus. It's .... the right as you go in.

4 The teaching block is .... the end of the road, facing the main entrance.

5 The main lecture theatre is .... the ground floor.

6 The library is .... the student union building, ... the left just after the entrance.

Now check your answers in the answer key.

5 Label the buildings on the plan with information from the sentences in exercise 4.

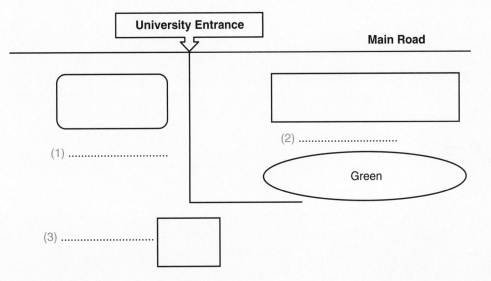

7 Studying, exams and revision

AIMS: Language related to: studying, exams and revision • Comparisons • *make / do*
• Adjectives and adverbs • Following processes • Completing sentences
• Completing flow charts • Short-answer questions

Part 1: Vocabulary

1 **Label the pictures with the words in the box.** revision   exam hall   test   text books

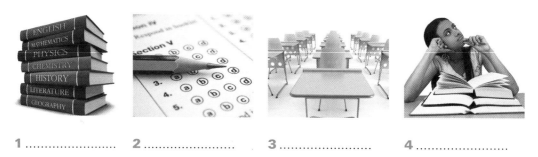

1 .... 2 .... 3 .... 4 ....

Comparatives

Look at these examples of comparative sentences:

The population of China is large. It is larger than the population of Italy.
Many students think physics is difficult. They say it is more difficult than art.
Spelling in Spanish is simple. At least, it's simpler than in English.
Some people think playing football is easy. They think it is easier than learning maths.
Exercising in the gym is good for your health, but it's even better to exercise in the fresh air.

Do you know all the different rules to form a comparative?

A	B	C	D	E
Adjectives with one syllable	**Adjectives with two or three syllables**	**Adjectives with two syllables and ending in '-le, -er', '-ow'**	**Adjectives with two syllables and ending in 'y'**	**Irregular adjectives**
add 'r' or 'er'	put 'more' in front of the adjective	add 'er'	add 'er' and change 'y' to 'i'	change spelling / into another word
large/larger strong/stronger	dif-fi-cult/more difficult bo-ring/more boring	simple/simpler	easy/easier	far/further

2 Form the comparative of these adjectives and write them in the correct column in the table below.

1 fast	**3** clever	**5** well	**7** late	**9** bad
2 interesting	**4** nervous	**6** slow	**8** healthy	**10** good

+ 'r'	+ 'er'	y + ier	more + adjective	irregular adjectives
	faster			

3 Now match your answers to the rules (A–E) in the table opposite. The first one has been done for you.

1 fast	…A…	**4** nervous	……….	**7** healthy	……….
2 interesting	……….	**5** slow	……….	**8** bad	……….
3 clever	……….	**6** late	……….	**9** good	……….

4 Complete the paragraph with words from the table in exercise 2. Use each word only once.

Some students think it is (1) …………… to study for exams at night, when it is quiet. Others think it is (2) …………… to go to bed early and get up early to do their exam revision. A lot of students enjoy studying (3) …………… subjects. Some like to revise at the last minute, but (4) …………… students need to plan their revision a long time in advance. Students who are (5) …………… than average before exams, can go to classes to learn relaxation techniques.

Adjectives and adverbs

Watch Out!

Be careful not to confuse adjectives with adverbs:
Adjectives tell us more about nouns. They come before the noun.
> *Amira is a confident speaker.*

Adverbs tell us more about verbs. They usually come after the verb.
> *Amira spoke confidently about her project on cultural exchanges.*

Adverbs can also tell us more about adjectives.
> *Amira is an exceptionally confident speaker.*

5 Choose the correct adjectives or adverbs to complete these sentences.

1 The (*intelligently / intelligent*) students answered the exam questions (*correct / correctly*).
2 A (*well / good*) designed exam tests the students' knowledge (*effectively / effective*).
3 The examiner marked the tests as (*fair / fairly*) and as (*quickly / quick*) as possible.
4 The coursework on the programme this year was (*unusual / unusually*) (*well / good*).
5 The students' projects have been of an (*extraordinary / extraordinarily*) (*high / highly*) standard.

Exam information | Sentence completion

In this type of task, for each question you will have to complete a sentence with words you hear on the recording. You must make sure that the answers are grammatically correct and that the spelling is accurate. You will only have to write two or three words or a number.

1 Look at the following sentences and endings. Choose the endings that are grammatically correct. In each question more than one answer is possible.

1 *Your exam revision will be more organized at the end of the year if*

  a you are planning a revision timetable.

  b you plan when to study each subject.

  c your revision is planning.

  d you have planned a revision timetable.

2 *Some subjects are easier to remember because*

  a they interesting.

  b they're interested.

  c they are interesting.

  d you're interested in them.

3 *If you study all night, because it's quieter,*

  a you'll be tired in the morning.

  b you're sleeping in your classes.

  c you might fall asleep in your lectures.

  d you'll be able to concentrate more.

Exam tip

When you are listening to a recording of several people talking, try to make a note of the names of the speakers when you hear them for the first time. It might help you to write just their initials and whether they are male or female.

For example: *A / f* (Amira – female) or *D / m* (Dave – male)

◀)) **2** Listen to this conversation about studying, and match the name of each person to the study
52 technique they prefer.

  1 Martha ………   **2** Carl ………   **3** Enrique ………   **4** Jenny ………

  A highlighting important details in photocopies of articles and text books

  B making notes in the margin of articles and text books writing notes in an exercise book

  C making notes in files on their PC

  D using free software to make notes on articles and electronic books

🔊 **3**
53

Now you will hear a group of students talking about their revision techniques and write the correct endings for each of the sentences. Write NO MORE THAN THREE WORDS.

1 Lesley prepares for her end-of-year exams by making a ....

2 Chen says that he can remember historical facts more easily if he creates pictures ....

3 Indira prefers to study late at night because it is ....

4 Mark likes to get up very early on the day of an exam to do some ....

🔊 **4**
54

Look at the pictures that show students what to do when they go for an exam. Listen to the recording and complete the instructions. Write NO MORE THAN THREE WORDS for each answer. Check that your answers are grammatically correct.

1 Leave your .... your bag.

2 The keys for the lockers are ....

3 Show your identity card ....

4 Look for your .... on a desk in the hall.

5

Look at these steps for preparing for an exam and put them in the order you would do them. There are several possible answers, but some are more practical than others. Don't check your answers yet.

A look at past exam papers **D** remember key facts and arguments

B read all the books on the subject **E** discuss possible exam topics with tutors

C write practice exam questions **F** look at all your lecture notes for the course

🔊 **6**
55

Now listen to three students talking about how they prepare for an exam and complete the flow chart with the missing letters from exercise 5.

(1) .... ⟹ (2) .... ⟹ D ⟹ (3) .... ⟹ (4) ....

Section 3

 01 **You will hear three students discussing exam techniques with their tutor. Complete the flow chart. Write no more than THREE words.**

Questions 1–4

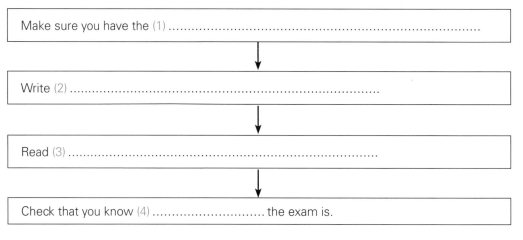

Make sure you have the (1) ....

Write (2) ....

Read (3) ....

Check that you know (4) .... the exam is.

 02 **Questions 5–8**

Now you will hear the next part of the recording. Complete the sentences. Write no more than THREE words for each answer.

5 You should read the questions .... to find out what the topic is.

6 Sometimes a question is .... than it looks.

7 It is a good idea to start by answering the questions you ....

8 When all the questions are worth the same .... you should check that you spend the right amount of time on them.

Questions 9–10

Listen to the last part of the recording and answer the questions. Write no more than THREE words or a number.

9 What should you write if you do not have time to give a complete answer to a question? ....

10 What did Barbara get in her last exam? ....

Progress check

How many boxes can you tick? You should work towards being able to tick them all.

Did you …

read all the questions before you listened to the recording? ☐

spell all your answers correctly? ☐

make sure your completed sentences were grammatically correct? ☐

keep to the word count? ☐

8 Shopping and spending

AIMS: Language related to shopping and spending habits • Predicting key words • Identifying opinions • Recognizing words that go together (collocations) • Completing notes • Matching information • Answering short-answer questions

Part 1: Vocabulary

Shopping options

1 Look at the pictures and match them with the sentences below.

a There are supermarkets in most big cities across the world. ....

b People who live in small towns often buy their food at the market. ....

c In the countryside, people often get their groceries in village shops. ....

d Department stores sell clothes, furniture and household goods. ....

2 Complete the sentences with the expressions from the box.

> designer brands   shop assistant   customer services
> shopping malls   market stalls   self-service

1 Ingrid complained to .... about her new boots because the zip was broken.

2 A lot of teenagers like expensive .... more than cheap clothes.

3 One advantage of .... is that you can choose your own food from the shelves.

4 Many young people in big cities go to .... to meet their friends.

5 Farmers often sell their fruit and vegetables from ....

6 The .... helped the customer to find a T shirt in the colour they wanted.

◀)) **3** Listen to the following sentences and underline the stressed words.
04

    1 I bought this shirt in a sale.

    2 My brother thinks online shopping is much quicker than going to the shops.

    3 The good thing about shopping in a department store is that you can get everything in one place.

    4 The last time I took something back to a shop, the customer services manager wasn't there.

    5 I lost my credit card the other day. I was really worried someone else would use it.

    6 Have you ever bought a train ticket with a student discount? It's so much cheaper.

Collocations

Some verbs go with certain nouns to form common expressions. For example: <u>make</u> + a phone call

4 Match the verbs with the nouns to form expressions about shopping.

1	go	**a**	the shopping
2	ask for	**b**	a shopping list
3	make	**c**	the supermarket
4	do	**d**	shopping
5	go to	**e**	a refund

◀)) **5** Now listen to a recording of an interview in a survey of shopping habits. Miriam is talking about
05 who does the shopping in her family. Complete the notes with the expressions from Exercise 1.

- Four people in the family – only two (1) ....

- Mother buys the food. Makes a (2) .... first.

  Goes to (3) .... weekly.

- Miriam (4) .... most. Sometimes buys clothes she

  doesn't like. Takes them back and asks for (5) ....

Exam information | Note completion

In this type of task, you will have to complete notes with words you hear on the recording. You will only have to write two or three words or a number. Listen carefully for words that tell you about the structure of the talk, for example, *first, next, now, finally*.

1 Look at these lists and circle any words that indicate the order of ideas in a talk. The first has been done for you.

1 in	as	though	(before)	however	(first)
2 over	then	through	next	such	near
3 secondly	there	so	because	finally	nevertheless
4 consequently	after	for	but	therefore	thirdly
5 lastly	that	prior to	since	also	never

2a The following notes are from a talk about shopping habits in different countries. Fill in the gaps with words you expect to hear.

Who does the shopping?

– In the UK (1) .... % food bought by women.

– In some countries (2) .... % men do grocery shopping.

– Habits changing – US (3) .... % of men shop for food.

Where do people shop?

– In cities (4) ....

– In country (5) .... and (6) ....

2b Now listen to the recording and check your answers.

06

Exam information | Multiple-choice questions

Before you answer multiple-choice questions, check that you know how many correct answers there are. In some cases, you have to choose *one* correct answer out of *three* possible options. In other questions you can choose *two* correct answers out of *five* options or *three* correct answers out of *seven* options.

🔊 **3**
07

You will hear a lecture about shopping habits. Choose THREE statements that are correct. Before you listen, make a note of what you *think* the answers might be.

What did the survey find out about women?

   a They like to shop in large department stores.

   b They go to the supermarket after midnight.

   c They always make a shopping list.

   d They tend to buy inexpensive shoes.

   e They save money by buying special offers.

   f They like expensive boutiques.

   g They go shopping in specialist shops.

1 ....

2 ....

3 ....

Exam Information | Short-answer questions

In another type of question you will have to give a short answer. Your answer does not have to be a complete sentence and you must not write more words that you are asked for. This is usually no more than TWO or THREE words. You will hear the exact words you have to write on the recording.

4

The instructions for this task tell you to write no more than THREE words. Look at these questions and their incorrect answers. Decide why the answers are incorrect and match the reasons.

   a too many words
   b not enough answers
   c misunderstood the question word

   d incorrect spelling
   e too many answers
   f misunderstood the question

	Question	Answer
1	Where do young people in the city like to meet their friends?	at the shopping mall
2	What three things do most teenagers like to spend their money on?	music, clothes, cinema, computers
3	How much does it cost to go to the cinema?	It is enjoyable.
4	What is the most expensive thing you have bought?	a mobbile phone
5	When do you go shopping?	to the supermarket
6	Name two places where you can buy food.	market stall

Exam tip

You will find clues about the topic of the talk in the instructions and the questions. Before you listen, read them carefully and think about the vocabulary you expect to hear.

Section 4

08

Questions 1–4

You will hear the introduction to a lecture about consumer habits. Complete the notes with **NO MORE THAN THREE WORDS AND/OR NUMBERS.**

Spending money

Point 1

– three age groups:

• young people,

• families,

• (1) ....

Point 2

– male and female (2) ....

Three age groups are

• Young people aged (3) ....

• Families aged from 30–55

• Mature adults (4) ....

Questions 5–7
09

Now you will hear the next part of the recording and answer the question. Select THREE correct options from the list (a–g).

What do families spend their money on?

a   furniture and household goods

b   clothes, music and entertainment

c   cars and outings

d   electronic equipment

e   gardening tools

f   food, toys and outings

g   cars and travelling

5   ....

6   ....

7   ....

Questions 8–10
10

Now you will hear the last part of the recording. Answer the questions. Write NO MORE THAN THREE WORDS OR A NUMBER for eating in restaurants.

8   What do men spend twice as much as women on?

....

9   What do women spend most on?

....

10   Which group spends most on eating in restaurants?

....

Progress check

How many boxes can you tick? You should work towards being able to tick them all.

Did you …

read the questions and think about the topic before you listened to the recording?

check all the options before you answered the matching question?

write the exact words you heard on the recording?

9 Hobbies, interests and sports

Part 1: Vocabulary

1

2

3

4

5

6

1a Look at the pictures. Copy and complete the table with the numbers of the pictures and the names of the activities.

Hobby	Interest	Sports
....	....	....
....	....	....

1b Now read the definitions below and check your answers.

Vocabulary note

A hobby is an activity you do for pleasure in your spare time. It often involves doing something with your hands or collecting something, for example, painting and collecting stamps are hobbies.

A *sport* is a game that involves physical activity.

An *interest* is something you enjoy doing. It may be a hobby, or a sport, but not always. For example, going to the cinema is an interest, but it is not a hobby or a sport.

Exam tip

Knowing that a word belongs to a group of words will make it easier for you to predict what you are going to hear in the recording. For example, if you know that *stamp collecting* is a *hobby*, you will be ready to listen for other words connected with hobbies.

2 **Put the following words in the correct column. Remember, hobbies and sports are interests, but not all interests are hobbies or sports.**

> playing chess   gardening   travelling   listening to music   football
> going to art galleries   running   cooking   swimming

Hobbies	Interests	Sports
stamp collecting	*going to the cinema*	*cycling*

3 **You will hear some people talking about what they are planning to do in their free time. Write the activity next to the speaker in each conversation. Check that your spelling is correct. Use only one word for each answer.**

11

Conversation A
Speaker 1: ....
Speaker 2: ....

Conversation B
Speaker 1: ....
Speaker 2: ....

Conversation C
Speaker 1: ....
Speaker 2: ....

Conversation D
Speaker 1: ....
Speaker 2: ....

Watch Out!

Spelling is important in the listening test. Remember that some words sound the same, but are written differently, for example *to, too and two*. When you hear these words, you will have to think about which one is grammatically possible.

4 **Complete these sentences with the correct spelling, *to, too* or *two*.**

1 Michael wants .... go travelling in the vacation.

2 Jeremy has .... much work to do.

3 Annie has .... sisters in Germany.

4 Edward is .... lazy to study for his exams.

5 Elizabeth would like to go .... Paris for the summer.

6 Faizal is planning .... vacations this year.

Exam tip

Some words can be confused because two letters may sound similar, for example: *p* and *b*, *l* and *r*. If you find these tricky, make sure you get plenty of practice before the exam.

🔊 **1**
12

Listen to the recording and circle the word you hear. You will hear the words twice.

1	*fly / fry*	6	*play / pray*
2	*play / pray*	7	*lead / read*
3	*lead / read*	8	*fly / fry*
4	*blade / played*	9	*blade / played*
5	*collect / correct*	10	*collect / correct*

🔊 **2**
13

Now you will hear a conversation between two people discussing their hobbies. Circle the words you hear.

1 *flying / frying / fly in*   3 *leading / reading / lead in*

2 *play / played / blade*

Exam information | Table completion

In this type of task, you will have to complete a table with information from the recording. Before you listen, read the headings of the columns in the table to see what kind of information you need to listen for. Remember to keep to the word count.

3 **This table shows how one person keeps a record of the stamps in their collection. Look at the headings in the table and make a note of what kind of information is required in each column, e.g. a number, a name, a date.**

Value	Picture	Year	Origin
(1)	*colour image*	(3)	(4)

🔊 **4**
14

You are going to hear a boy talking to a friend about his stamp collection. Listen and complete the table about the stamps. Write NO MORE THAN TWO WORDS OR A NUMBER.

Value	Picture	Year	Origin
32 cents	cardinal honeyeater	(1)	(2) ....
25 cents	parrot	(3)	(4) ....

Exam information | Completing forms

In this type of question you will often need to listen for numbers and letters. These might be part of an address, name, age or phone number. Before you listen, read the form carefully. It will give you a lot of clues about the topic of the recording and the kind of information you will need.

5 Before you hear a student applying to join a mountain climbing club, read the list of questions below and make a note of the kind of information you need.

Question	Type of information
1 Are you over 18?	*age*
2 Where do you live?	
3 What's your family name?	
4 Do you have a number where I can contact you?	
5 Do you have any health problems?	
6 Do you have any climbing experience?	

6 Now you will hear a young man talking to the administrator of a climbing club. Complete his application form.

15

Mountain High Climbing Club

Membership Application form

Name: (1) ....

Age: (2) ....

Address: (3) .... Highbury Square, LONDON, W1

Telephone number: 07209 (4) ....

Health problems: **No**

Previous experience: (*circle one*) (5) none / some / extensive

Section 1

16

Questions 1–4

You will hear two students talking about university clubs and societies. Complete the table.
Write NO MORE THAN TWO WORDS OR A NUMBER.

Club	Membership fee	Number of members
(1)	£20	60
cross country cycling	£15	(2) ....
film and drama	£50	(3) ....
(4)	£5	80

17

Questions 5–7

Now you will hear the next part of the recording. Choose THREE letters a–g.

Which THREE activities does Victoria enjoy?

    a   contemporary dance

    b   yoga

    c   film and drama

    d   cycling

    e   photography

    f   running

    g   jazz and tap dancing

    5 ....

    6 ....

    7 ....

🔊 **Questions 8–10**

18

Listen to the last part of the recording and complete the form. Write no more than TWO words or a number.

Club Membership Application form

University
Club

(tick relevant clubs)

athletics	☐	pilates	☐
baseball	☐	running	☐
basketball	☐	sailing	☐
chess	☐	snooker	☐
contemporary dance	☐	street dance	☐
cycling	☐	swimming	☐
kick boxing	☐	table tennis	☐
parachuting	☐	yoga	☐
photography	☐		

Name: (8) Victoria ....

Age: 19

Address: (9) 57, ..., Atherton Park, MANCHESTER, M46

Contact number: (10) ....

Email: victoriainatherton@england.com

Progress check

How many boxes can you tick? You should work towards being able to tick them all.

Did you …
check that you gave the right number of answers?   ☐
revise the pronunciation of the letters of the alphabet?   ☐
think about the spelling of words that sound the same?   ☐

Review 3

1 Complete the sentences with the correct comparatives from the brackets.

1 Revising for exams was (easy) .... than Carl expected.

2 The students thought the seminar would last (long) .... than an hour.

3 The final examination was the (tough) .... of all.

4 Mathematics was the (bad) .... of Tom's exams.

5 The tutor noticed that his students studied (well) .... in the afternoon.

6 Michael got the (good) .... mark in the class for his coursework.

2 Change the following adjectives into comparisons.

1	slow	......*slower*........	6	healthy	....
2	pretty	....	7	near	....
3	clever	....	8	hard	....
4	good	....	9	early	....
5	difficult	....	10	boring	....

3 Complete the table below with words from the box that have similar meanings.

sale price	store	bargain	style	items	supermarket
articles	deal	design	produce	reduction	market

Shop	Discount	Fashion	Goods
	sale price		

4 Listen and answer with as many words as you feel are necessary. Then look at the corresponding audio script on page 109 and reduce your answers to two words. Underline the words you choose. Check them in the answer key.

🔊
19

 1 Who did the speaker think would spend most on electronic equipment?
 ....

 2 What do young men spend more on? ....

 3 What are people between 30 and 55 buying their household equipment for?
 ....

5 Read these instructions and underline the key words.

 1 You are going to hear two people talking about where they are going on holiday. Listen and complete the sentences. Write NO MORE THAN TWO WORDS AND/OR A NUMBER.

 2 Listen to this recording of a student asking about how to join a club. Complete the form. Write NO MORE THAN TWO WORDS in each space.

 3 Listen to the recording of two students talking about their hobbies. Complete the notes. Write NO MORE THAN THREE WORDS AND/OR A NUMBER.

 4 You are going to hear a woman talking to a friend about her weekend. Listen and match the woman's opinion with the different activities.

 5 You are going to hear two people discussing their favourite film. Listen and choose the correct answer from the list (A–C).

6 What kind of information would you expect to hear in the recordings in exercise 5? Complete the table with words from the following groups. You can use each word more than once. The first one has been done for you.

comparisons   stories   ages   prices   weather   names   phone numbers
seasons   addresses   months   activities   days   transport   types of film
times   dates   countries   cities hotels   hobbies   actors   sports

1	2	3	4	5
dates prices weather seasons times months activities transport countries cities hotels				

10 Work-life balance

Part 1: Vocabulary

1   2   3   4

1 In this unit we will look at work-life balance. This is the way we use and manage our time, when we are working or studying. Which of the words below do you relate with the photos? There are more words than pictures.

> career   relaxation   stress   factory   employer   deadline   study

1 ....   2 ....   3 ....   4 ....

Words that have similar meanings

2 Circle the words in each list that do <u>not</u> have a similar meaning to the others.

1 career	job	hobby	profession	occupation
2 relaxation	leisure	rest	holidays	work
3 stress	worry	difficulty	pressure	comfort
4 factory	beach	office	shop	workshop
5 employer	boss	owner	worker	manager
6 deadline	limit	goal	target	start

Noun or verb?

3 Some of the words in exercise 2 are nouns and some are nouns <u>and</u> verbs. Copy and complete the table with the words from lists A, B and C. Use a dictionary to check your answers.

Noun	Noun and verb
career	

4 Although the words in exercise 3 have similar meanings, they are not exactly the same. Complete the following sentences with the best word from the table.

1 Margaret decided to apply for a new .... to earn more money.
2 The college gave the teachers longer .... so they could spend more time with their families.
3 When they are studying for exams, students .... that they will not be able to remember all the important facts.
4 The college organized a day off for the .... staff.
5 The .... of the factory invested in a new building for storing supplies.
6 Students are expected to meet the .... for handing in their work.

Spelling

Watch Out!

Capital letters are part of spelling. You will lose marks in the exam if you do not use capital letters correctly. You should use capitals for:

- the names of countries, towns and cities
- the names of nationalities, religions and languages
- months and days of the week
- the names of institutions and organizations

5 Write the following sentences with the correct punctuation in your notebook.

1 new york is not the Capital of the united states of America.
2 in the uk, children who are born in july usually start school in September, just after they are five
3 oxford university is one of the most famous in the World.
4 in some countries, most companies close on sundays, but in others they close on fridays or saturdays
5 the official language of greece is greek

Exam information | Sentence completion

In this type of task, you will have to complete sentences with words you hear on the recording. Your answers must be grammatically correct and you must keep to the word count. Look for clues to the answers in the sentences you have to complete. For example, if the word before the gap is *an*, you should listen carefully for words beginning with a vowel (a, e, i, o, u).

The final *s*

While you are listening to the recording, remember to listen for the final *s* in verbs, possessives and plural nouns.

- Make sure that the subject of the sentence (a noun) matches the verb. For example, in the present simple tense, singular nouns (e.g. the names of people, places, groups, objects) must be followed by a verb with a final *s*.

- Also remember that the final *s* in a plural word may be pronounced together with first part of the next word, and be difficult to hear. So you will also need to listen closely to the endings of the verbs.

- The final *s* is also used at the end of a word to show that something belongs to someone. For example: My sister's children stay with me during the holidays. (one sister) My sisters' children stay with me during the holidays. (more than one sister)

◀») **1**
20

Listen to the recording and look at the answers to this sentence completion question. Which answer is correct?

Their .... at the beginning of July.

i *Their holiday starts at the beginning of July. (singular)*
ii *Their holidays start at the beginning of July. (plural)*

We know (i) is singular because the verb '*starts*' ends with an '*s*' and we know (ii) is plural because the verb '*start*' doesn't end with an '*s*'.

2

21

Now you will hear a lecturer giving some students advice on how to balance their studies and their free time. Select the correct completed sentences.

i   **a**   *So you'll have to do a lot more things for yourself,* like buying your own food, washing your clothes and managing your own money

    b   *So you'll have to do lots more things for yourself,* like buying your own food, washing your clothes and managing your own money

ii   **a**   At university you won't have as many hours *of class.*

    b   At university you won't have as many hours *of classes.*

iii   **a**   Actually, your university might even have a system for alerting you on your mobile *when your lecture is.*

    b   Actually, your university might even have a system for alerting you on your mobile *when your lectures are.*

iv   **a**   One thing I will say, though, is that at the end of the year, *after your exam, you can really relax.*

    b   One thing I will say, though, is that at the end of the year, *after your exams, you can really relax.*

Exam tip

If you don't know the meaning of a word, don't worry. Focus on the words around it. They will give you an idea of the topic and the situation and will help you decide whether it is a key word. If it _is_ important, try to guess the meaning from the situation. If it isn't, don't waste any time.

3

22

You are going to hear a recording of a new employee describing the problems she has with time management. Listen and complete the sentences with words from the text. Write no more than THREE WORDS or a NUMBER.

1   In her previous job, the speaker worked from .... to
    ....
2   In her new job, employees are allowed to
    .... the office between 8.00 and 10.00 in the morning.
3   If the employees .... a lunch break they can go home between 3.00 and 5.00 pm.
4   .... she goes to the gym in the morning.
5   The children .... of school at 4.00.

4 You will hear a market researcher describing how he plans a project. Before you listen, look at the possible labels for the diagram (A–G) and choose alternative expressions from the list (1–7).

Labels		Alternative expressions	
A	deadline	1	part
B	tasks	2	step in a process
C	finishing line	3	final date for completion
D	section	4	end of a race
E	start date	5	important achievements
F	milestones	6	beginning
G	phase	7	activities

🔊 **5** Now listen to the market researcher describing how he plans a project. Label the diagram below. Choose FIVE answers from the box and write the correct letters A–G next to the questions.

23

A Deadline
B Tasks
C Finishing line
D Section
E Start date
F Milestones
G Completion of phase 1

(1)	(2)	(3)				(4)	(5) ....
Team meeting	23/01	15/02	18/03	25/04	30/06	15/08	15/09
Draft questionnaire		■	■				
Check questionnaire			■	■			
Complete survey					■		
Enter data on database						■	
Phase 1							
Write report							■

Part 3: Exam practice

Questions 1–5

You will hear a human resource manager talking about her company's work-life balance policy. Complete the sentences. Write **NO MORE THAN TWO WORDS OR A NUMBER**.

1 The company is concerned about the physical .... health of the workers.
2 It aims to give employees a chance to create a balance between their work and .... lives.
3 Some parents need to work .... hours so they can look after their children.
4 A lot of parents work part time and others work ....
5 Women who have had a baby can take .... off work before they come back to the office.

Questions 6–8

Listen to the next part of the recording and label the pie chart. Write **NO MORE THAN THREE WORDS OR A NUMBER**.

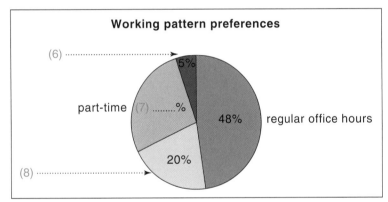

Working pattern preferences

(6) ....
5%
part-time (7) ....%
48%   regular office hours
20%
(8) ....

Questions 9–10

Listen to the last part of the recording and complete the notes. Write **NO MORE THAN THREE WORDS OR A NUMBER**.

Sally has (9) .... Leaves them at nursery before 8.00 a.m.
Collects them from (10) .... house in the afternoon. Finishes her work at home.

Progress check

How many boxes can you tick? You should work towards being able to tick them all.

Did you …
listen for the final *s* in verbs, plural nouns and possessives?
check that your answers were grammatically accurate?
use capital letters correctly?

11 Comparing cultures

Part 1: Vocabulary

Cultures across the world

1 2 3 4

1 Use the pictures above and the clues to complete the word puzzle.

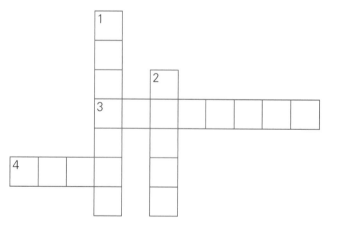

Across:

3 This little girl is wearing her .... costume.

4 In villages in Africa and South America, many people live in .... like these.

Down:

1 This is an example of .... writing.

2 This is the national dish of ....

2 Complete the word maps on the opposite page with words from the box below.

scarf   vegetarian   spicy   pronunciation   silk   brick   block of flats   alphabet

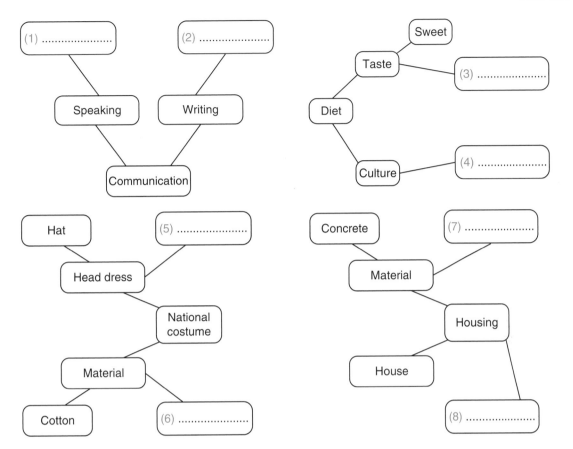

Listening for key words

🔊 **3** You will hear four conversations between students discussing their projects on world
27 cultures. Circle the topic of each conversation from the key words in the word map.

     A language, dress, housing, diet   **C** clothes, festivals, homes, communication

     B costume, housing, culture, literature   **D** communication, food, costume, art

🔊 **4** Listen again and write, in your notebook, any words from the word maps that are mentioned.
27

5 The verbs *make*, *have* and *do* are often confused. Circle the correct verb.

    1 Every year in April we (*make / have / do*) a Water Festival.

    2 Recently, our country has (*made / had / done*) progress in improving education.

    3 In some places tourism has (*made / had / done*) a lot of damage to the environment.

    4 Global warming has (*made / had / done*) a negative effect on many rare animals.

    5 In the spring, we (*make/ have / do*) a lot of work in the garden.

    6 When people get married, they (*make / have / do*) a big party to celebrate.

Listening for comparisons and contrasts

Compare means to look at things to see how they are <u>similar</u> and how they are <u>different</u>.
Contrast means to look at things to see how they are <u>different</u>.

🔊 **1**
28

You will hear a conversation between a tutor and a student about a project on how much people talk in public in different countries. Underline the comparing and contrasting words that you hear in the conversation.

the same as   different from   more [adjective] than   much more [adjective]
in comparison with   [adjective] ....er than   like

We often use other words with comparisons to emphazise or limit any similarity.

For example: The pronunciation of Spanish in South America is <u>not exactly the same as</u> the pronunciation of Spanish in Spain.

This means that the pronunciation of Spanish in South America is <u>similar in some ways</u> to the pronunciation of Spanish in Spain, <u>but not in others</u>.

2   **Copy and complete the table with the words in the box. The first one has been done for you.**

> ~~very~~   a bit   extremely   incredibly   quite   not   a little   exactly   rather

To emphazise similarity	To limit similarity
very	

We also use words like *and*, *as well as*, *too* to show that things are similar, for example:

Rice is popular in India <u>as well as</u> in China.
Rice is popular in India and in China, <u>too</u>.

We use words like *but*, *except*, *apart from* to show that things are different, for example:

Most houses in the UK are made of brick, <u>but</u> blocks of flats are made of concrete.
Many homes in the UK are made of brick, <u>except / apart from</u> blocks of flats, which are made of concrete.

Exam Information | Multiple-choice – matching information

In this type of question you will have to match information in the recording with different speakers. You have to choose from several options, but you will not hear them in the same order as they appear on the question sheet. Make sure you read all the options before you listen to the recording.

🔊 **3** You will hear three people discussing eating habits in their home countries. Choose THREE
29 letters (a–g). Listen carefully for the relevant part of the conversation.

Match the country where they eat this food for lunch.

a potatoes	**d** noodle soup	**g** chicken
b cereal toast and eggs	**e** rice and vegetables	
c bread with lentils	**f** a sandwich	

1 in the UK .... **2** in India .... **3** in China ....

Exam tip

In this type of multiple-choice question, try turning the first half of the sentence, or
sentence stem, into a question. It might help you find the right answer.

4 Turn these sentence stems into questions.

1 In traditional Indian families the bride and groom meet for the first time at …

....

2 In India the father of the bride used to …

....

3 Recently it has become very popular for Indian families to …

....

4 After they are married the couple live …

....

🔊 **5** Listen to two students comparing marriage customs in their countries and choose a, b or c.
30

i In traditional Indian families the bride and groom used to meet for the first time at the

  a marriage.   **b** girl's home.   **c** boy's home.

ii In India, the father of the bride used to give the

  a bride a gift.   **b** groom some money.   **c** groom's family a gift.

iii Recently it has become popular for Indian families to

  a use websites to find marriage partners for their children.

  b ask their children to get married online.

  c send their children abroad to find a partner.

iv These days, in India, more and more married couples live

  a with the girl's family.

  b on their own.

  c with the groom's family.

> ## Exam tip
>
> Listen to the introduction to each recording. It will give you an idea of what the conversation will be about. You will have time at the beginning of the test, and between each recording, to read the questions and think about possible answers.

Section 3

🔊
31

Questions 1–2

You will hear two students discussing a project on international festivals with their tutor. Complete the sentences with the correct answer from the list.

1 The students are planning to study

    a different types of celebration.

    b how the festivals started.

    c people's attitudes to festivals.

2 The students have already discovered

    a the seasons in different countries.

    b how the Carnival is linked to different times of the year.

    c similarities between countries that are far away from each other.

🔊
32

Questions 3–5

Now you will hear the next part of the recording. Choose THREE letters (a–g).

What do the students say about the changes in the Carnival since it started?

    a It has turned into a church celebration.

    b It celebrates the end of winter.

    c It is only celebrated in Europe.

    d It is celebrated in many different regions.

    e It takes place during the rainy season.

    f It is not connected with the seasons.

    g It is celebrated when the weather is very hot.

    3 what   ....

    4 where   ....

    5 when   ....

Questions 6–10

🔊
33

Listen to the next part of the recording and answer the questions. Write no more than
THREE WORDS OR A NUMBER.

6   What else are the students going to research?

    ....

7   How many countries do they know of where festivals involve water?

    ....

8   What three meanings can water have?

    ....

9   What do water festivals celebrate?

    ....

10 How are the Carnival and the seasons linked?

    ....

Progress check

How many boxes can you tick? You should work towards being able to tick them all.

Did you …
turn the first half of the sentences into questions?   ☐
listen for phrases that compare and contrast?   ☐
listen to the introductions to the recordings?   ☐

12 Exploring the oceans

AIMS: Language related to: words about ocean life, natural resources, minerals, exploration, statistics • Predicting answers from context • Identifying key words • Recognizing steps in a process • Understanding statistics • Completing diagrams and flow charts • Completing notes

Part 1: Vocabulary

1 Each picture shows a different way of using the ocean. Copy and complete the table with the following words and phrases. Some can go into more than one column.

> oil rig   natural gas   trawler   mineral resource   off-shore drilling   fish farm
> underwater turbine   wave power   gas pipeline   energy   fuel   net

Picture 1	Picture 2	Picture 3	Picture 4
oil rig			

2 Match the phrases with the definitions.

1	off-shore drilling	a	a large structure for drilling for oil from the sea bed
2	wave power	b	a material that is burned to produce power
3	mineral	c	a type of fishing boat
4	fuel	d	a natural material
5	trawler	e	energy generated from the movement of the sea
6	rig	f	a method of extracting oil from the sea bed

Watch Out!

Remember, spelling is important in the Listening test. Listen carefully even when you think you know the words. Their spelling may depend on their meaning in the recording.

3 Circle the correct spellings in the following sentences.

    1 Oil is a non-renewable *sauce / source* of power.

    2 Fishing boats often spend many months at *see / sea*.

    3 The melting ice-caps have *affected / effected* the level of the oceans.

    4 *Are / Our* knowledge of the deepest parts of the ocean is increasing.

    5 Wave power is generated when waves *break / brake* on the shore.

    6 Ocean *currants / currents* control the weather across the globe.

Trends and statistics

Statistics are the numbers which record facts (like the number of births and deaths in a year) and words that describe these numbers in relation to the whole group.

> *113 fishing boats were lost at sea last year.*
> *20% of the fish population is currently at risk of disappearing.*
> *The majority of our electricity could be generated by wave power.*

Trends describe *patterns of change* in social behaviour or environmental conditions over a period of time and may tell us how much they have changed.

> *Since 2009, interest in wave power has increased significantly.*
> *There has been a **dramatic rise** in fish farming **over the last ten years**.*
> *During this century there has been an upward trend in global temperatures.*

4 Do the following graphs show trends or statistics? Match the statements with the charts.

    1 The number of destructive storms has increased significantly in the last ten years.

    2 There has been a gradual rise in the temperature across the globe recently.

    3 The polar bear population has fallen dramatically since 2010.

    4 The frequency of volcanic eruptions has remained stable over the past century.

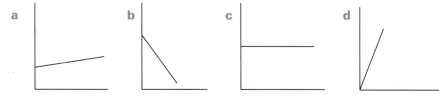

5 The following expressions are used to describe *statistics* and *trends*. Copy and complete the table, and say whether they are nouns, verbs, adjectives or adverbs. The first one has been done for you.

> rise   average   gradual   per cent   more than   fall   majority
> increase decrease minority   remain stable   less than   downward   fraction
> upward number   slight   tendency   amount   significant   dramatic

Statistics	Trends
....	*rise (noun/verb)* ....

Exam tip

When you do not know the meaning of a word, try to guess by listening for:

- the structure of the word: Is it a noun (e.g. ending in: *–ion, –ship, –ment, –er, –ist*) or an adjective (e.g., ending in: *–able, –ful, –ive*) or a verb (past or present tense)?
- the words that come before and after, e.g. an article, an adjective, etc.
- the context or meaning of the words that surround the word.
- words that sound similar, e.g. *horticulture* sounds a little like *agriculture* and might make you think about *growing* or *farming*.

1 **Look at this example. Guess the meaning of the underlined words and write them in your notebook. Then check your answers.**

The <u>bathysphere</u> allowed scientists to explore deeper areas of the ocean bed.

We know that 'bathysphere' is a noun because it has 'the' in front of it, and is followed by a 'verb'. We can guess that it is a piece of equipment because it helped scientists to study the sea bed and we can guess that it is no longer in use because the verb 'allowed' is in the past tense.

1 New <u>submarine</u> technologies are opening up the sea bed for exploration.
2 Fixed oil rigs can only be built in <u>shallow</u> water because they rest on the sea bed.
3 <u>Aquaculture</u> has developed significantly over the last 50 years, and now provides 40% of the world's fish.
4 A historic <u>descent</u> to the ocean floor has <u>revealed</u> the existence of mysterious <u>marine</u> creatures that look like huge prawns.

2 **Now put the underlined into the correct column according to their use in these examples.**

Noun	Adjective	Verb

Exam information | Labelling diagrams

When you are asked to label a visual, such as a diagram, map or a set of pictures, or complete a flow chart, you may have to select the correct answers from a list of options, or you may have to select words from the recording and keep to a specified word limit.

🔊 **3** Listen to the talk about the structure of an offshore oil rig and label the diagram.
34

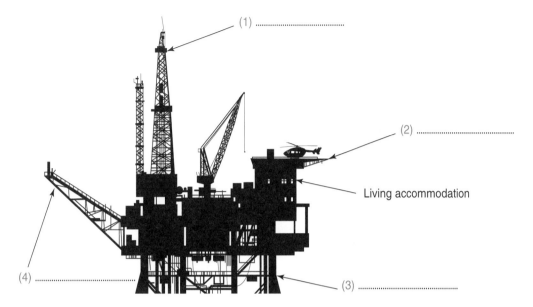

(1) ....

(2) ....

Living accommodation

(4) ....

(3) ....

🔊 **4** You will hear an engineer talking about using the sea to generate electricity. Complete the
35 values for the capacity in megawatts in the years below (**1–4**). Then plot the points on the
graph and draw the trend line.

1 2008 ....   **2** 2009 ....   **3** 2012 ....   **4** 2014 ....

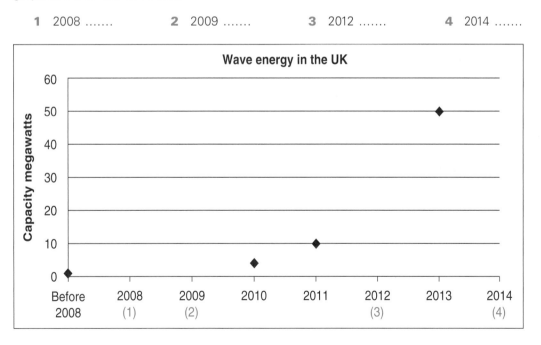

Exam information | Labelling diagrams

In this type of exercise, you will hear the information on the recording in the same order as the numbers on the answer sheet. Before you listen, look at the diagram and notice the position of the numbers. Underline any information you have about the diagram, including the parts that are already labelled.

Section 4

🔊 36

Questions 1–4

You will hear a recording of a lecture on deep sea exploration. Listen to the first part of the lecture and complete the time line using **NO MORE THAN TWO WORDS AND/OR NUMBERS FROM THE RECORDING.**

| Diving Bell invented | Diving Bell descended to (1) .... | Bathyscaphe invented | Trieste descended to 10,000 metres | Cameron descended to (4) .... |

| 1920s | 1934 | | | 2012 |

(2) ....   (3) ....

🔊 37

Questions 5–8

Now you will hear the next part of the lecture. Label the diagram of the Deep Sea Challenger. WRITE NO MORE THAN THREE WORDS.

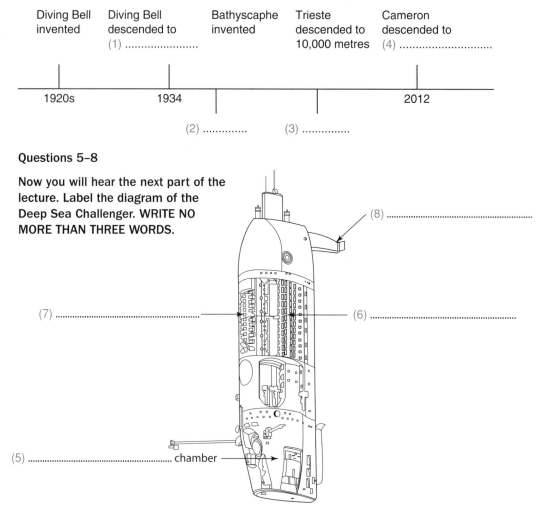

(8) ....

(7) ....

(6) ....

(5) .... chamber

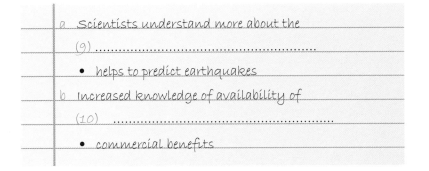

Questions 9–10

Now listen to the final part of the lecture and complete the notes. WRITE NO MORE THAN THREE WORDS OR A NUMBER.

Justifications for deep sea research:

> a Scientists understand more about the
>
> (9) ....
>
> • helps to predict earthquakes
>
> b Increased knowledge of availability of
>
> (10) ....
>
> • commercial benefits

Progress check

How many boxes can you tick? You should work towards being able to tick them all.

Did you …

check the spelling of words that may be confused? ☐

try to guess the meaning of the words you did not understand by
   listening carefully to the words that came before and after them? ☐

read the titles and key words on the diagrams before you listened? ☐

Review 4

1 Rewrite these sentences in your notebook, with the correct capital letters and punctuation.

1 is gardening a hobby or a sport

2 several thousand people ran in the london marathon in 2012

3 south america is a very large continent with a variety of climates

4 hindi is the official language of india

5 an australian accent is not the same as a new zealand one

6 the capital of the united states is not new york, but washington dc

7 oxford university is one of the best in the world

8 in many large companies employees work from monday to friday and some even work on saturdays

2 Listen to the recording and underline the word or phrase you hear in each sentence.

39

1 *study / studies*   4 *class / classes*

2 *thanks / thank*   5 *country / countries*

3 *languages / language*   6 *communication / communications*

3 Underline the correct word to complete the following sentences.

1 When we are learning a new language we (*make / do / have*) a lot of mistakes.

2 It is the custom in England to (*make / do / have*) a party when someone has a birthday.

3 Carefully regulated tourism does not (*make / do / have*) the environment any harm.

4 When people get married they sometimes (*make / do / have*) a week off work to go on honeymoon.

5 People may speak the same language, but depending on the country, some words may (*make / do / have*) a different pronunciation.

6 The travel agent (*made / had / did*) a hotel booking for the tourists.

7 Due to conservation policies, a few rare animals in China (*make / do / have*) a good chance of survival.

8 In hot climates many homes (*make / have / do*) air-conditioning.

4   **Complete these sentences with the correct form of the comparison.**

1   Most people think that their home country is (beautiful) .... any other.
2   It is much (easy) .... to learn a language that is nearly (same)
.... your own than one that is completely different.
3   The diet in Europe is much (greasy) .... the diet in Asia.
4   Experiencing new cultures is much (exciting) .... staying in one place all
your life.
5   The north of India is not nearly (hot) .... the south.
6   Marriage customs in the Middle East are rather (conservative) .... in Europe.
7   England is not quite (cold) .... Scotland.

5   **Complete these sentences with words from the box. You may have to modify their form.**

source / sauce	sea / see	descent / decent
affect / effect	currents / currants	accept / except

1   .... are dried grapes.
2   Sailors spend the majority of their working lives at ....
3   The temperature of the ocean has been .... by global warming.
4   The UK energy industry is beginning to .... the importance of wave and
tidal power
5   .... for two men, no one has travelled to the ocean bed in the Mariana Trench.
6   Rain is the main .... of fresh water on the planet.
7   The water in the ocean flows in .... which carry fish and marine life from
one side of the world to the other.
8   The .... from the surface of the ocean to the deepest part takes just over
an hour.

6   **Copy and complete the table by putting the following words into the correct columns.**

marine	majority	gradually	hatch	descent	descend	submarine
exploration research	scientifically	mystery	mysterious	scientist	technology
significantly	reveal	revelation	shallow	explore	technological

Noun	Adjective	Verb	Adverb

Practice test

Section 1

40

Questions 1–3

Answer the questions below. Choose the correct letter, a, b or c.

Example: How long does the caller want to go away for?

    a   a week   **b**   a few weeks   **c**   a few days

1   Where does the caller want to stay?

    a   in the country   **c**   by the beach

    b   in the city

2   What kind of hotel does the caller want to stay in?

    a   a family hotel   **c**   a farmhouse

    b   a spa

3   Which hotel does the caller choose?

    a   Sparkling Springs   **c**   Ocean Waves Resort

    b   Farmhouse Getaways

41

Questions 4–7

Complete the form below. Write **NO MORE THAN THREE WORDS AND/OR A NUMBER** for each answer.

Hotel Reservation Form	
Name:	William French
Billing Address:	(4) .... Standmarch Norfolk NE1 4SP
Mobile Number:	(5) ....
Check-in Date:	15th June
Check-out Date:	(6) ....
Payment Type:	Credit card
Amount:	(7) £...

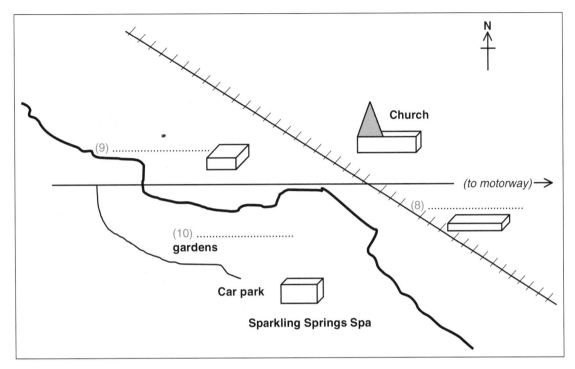

Questions 8–10

Complete the map below. Write NO MORE THAN THREE WORDS AND/OR A NUMBER for each answer.

Section 2

Questions 11–13

Answer the questions below. Write NO MORE THAN THREE WORDS AND/OR A NUMBER for each answer.

11 Which exhibition does the tour guide recommend? ....

12 How long do the guided tours last? ....

13 On which floor do the tours start? ....

Questions 14–17

Match the sections of the museum with the age group they are recommended for. Write A–C next to 14–17.

> **A** young people
> **B** adults
> **C** children

14 shapes and patterns ....
15 the history of flight ....
16 energy ....
17 exploring physics ....

45

Questions 18–20

Complete the flow chart below. Write **NO MORE THAN THREE WORDS AND/OR A NUMBER** for each answer.

How to buy a ticket for an exhibition:

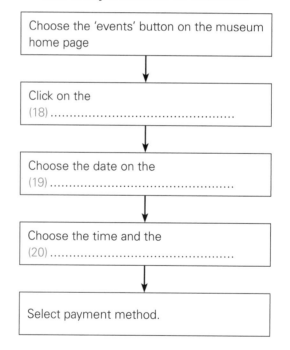

Choose the 'events' button on the museum home page

↓

Click on the (18) ....

↓

Choose the date on the (19) ....

↓

Choose the time and the (20) ....

↓

Select payment method.

Section 3

46

Questions 21–23

Complete the notes below. Write NO MORE THAN THREE WORDS AND/OR A NUMBER for each answer.

Focus of survey: (21) .... preferences

Number of questions: 20

Information required in first three questions: cost, number of rooms and
(22) ....

Topic of additional information: (23) ....

47

Questions 24–26

Choose THREE letters a–g

Which THREE ways does the tutor suggest Monica and Tom can improve their questionnaire?

a   make the questions shorter

b   make the questions simpler

c   increase the number of questions

d   ask more questions about the students' homes

e   not to ask so many questions

f   ask for more explanations

g   ask more questions about cost

24   ....

25   ....

26   ....

48

Questions 27–30

Complete the diagram below. Write NO MORE THAN THREE WORDS AND/OR A NUMBER for each answer.

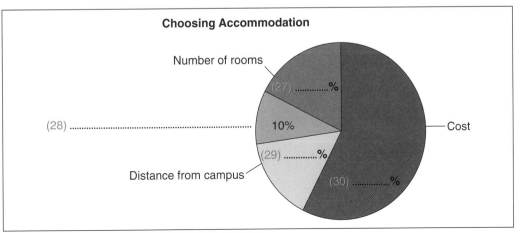

Choosing Accommodation

Number of rooms — (27) ....%

(28) ....

10%

Cost

(29) ....%

Distance from campus

(30) ....%

Section 4

Questions 31–34

Complete the summary of the introduction to a lecture on bird migration below. Write NO MORE THAN THREE WORDS AND/OR A NUMBER for each answer.

Birds migrate for two main reasons: to (31) .... and to breed. When they are breeding they need to move to areas where they can (32) .... In the spring they migrate from (33) .... to cooler countries in the north. They spend several months there, flying south again in the winter to (34) ....

Questions 35–37

Answer the questions below. Write NO MORE THAN THREE WORDS AND/OR A NUMBER for each answer.

35 How has global warming affected the arrival of spring? ....

36 Why have birds started to migrate earlier? ....

37 What happens to the population of birds that breed late? ....

Questions 38–40

Choose THREE letters A–F

Match each geographical area with a migration pattern.

> **A** migration to warm countries
> **B** clockwise migration
> **C** long distance migration
> **D** partial migration
> **E** migration to countries with long days
> **F** circular migration around entire globe

38 the tropics ....
39 the Arctic and Antarctic ....
40 North America ....

Audio scripts

Some sections of the audio scripts are underlined. This is to help you by pointing out the relevant information that corresponds to the correct answers.

Unit 1   Friends abroad

Track 01

Travel agent:	Good morning. Hi Fliers, can I help you?
Taxi driver:	Hello, Margaret. This is Dave. I'm at the airport and I want to check the flights of the passengers I'm meeting.
Travel agent:	Oh, OK, Dave. Go ahead.
Taxi driver:	Right. <u>The Spanish flight arrived at 04.50</u> and <u>flight 1550 from China</u> arrived at 6.00. The 6.50 from the Emirates, has been delayed. <u>That's flight UAE1880</u>, but the <u>Lisbon flight's already landed at Terminal 16.</u> Is that all of them? And do you have any news about …

Gate

Track 02

Ali:	Hello?
Sam:	Hello. Is that Ali?
Ali:	Yes. Who's calling?
Sam:	Hi Ali. It's me, Sam!
Ali:	Hey, Sam. How are you? When are you arriving?
Sam:	I'm fine. Really looking forward to seeing you. I've booked my flight for Wednesday morning, <u>arriving at 6.50 in the evening</u>.
Ali:	Great! That's <u>Wednesday 6th July</u>. And what airline are you flying on?
Sam:	<u>British Airways</u>, flight number <u>BA3025</u>
Ali:	BA1325?
Sam:	No. Three oh two five. 30-25.
Ali:	Ah … OK. And it gets in at 6.15, right?
Sam:	No. At 6.50. Ten to seven.
Ali:	Right. Sorry, this line's not very good. So you'll be on flight BA3025 on Wednesday 6th arriving at 6.50 p.m.
Sam:	That's right.
Ali:	Good. Well, don't worry. I'll be there to meet you at the airport. We're going to have a fantastic time. I can show you …

Track 03

18, 13, 80, 40, 15

Track 04

1   The youngest passenger is sitting in seat <u>fourteen</u>, by the window.

2   There are <u>forty</u> passengers in first class.
3   There should be <u>fifty</u> people on the bus.
4   Her plane arrives at <u>sixteen fifteen</u>.
5   Our train leaves at <u>seventeen thirty</u>.

Track 05

Restaurant manager:	Good evening, Fine Dining, can I help you?
Mr McEwan:	Hello, yes. I'd like to book a table for four on Friday evening at 8 p.m.
Restaurant manager:	Yes, sir. And the name is?
Mr McEwan:	<u>McEwan… M-C-E-W-A-N.</u>
Restaurant manager:	M-C-E-W-A-N, is that right, sir?
Mr McEwan:	Yes, that's right.
Restaurant manager:	That's booked for you sir. Four people on Friday night at 8 o'clock.

Track 06

Taxi driver:	Where to, madam?
Passenger:	Westbourne Grove, please.
Taxi driver:	Westerborne Grove, in the city centre?
Passenger:	No. <u>Westbourne</u>, near the park. Sorry, I haven't got the postcode.
Taxi driver:	No problem. How do you spell it?
Passenger:	<u>W-E-S-T-B-O-U-R-N-E</u>

Track 07

Receptionist:	Good morning. Taxis 4U. How can I help you?
Sam:	Oh, good morning. I'd like to book a taxi to the airport, please.
Receptionist:	Right … and which airport is that?
Sam:	London Heathrow.
Receptionist:	That's fine. And when do you need the taxi for?
Sam:	My flight leaves from terminal 5 at 7.20 on Wednesday 6th July. Next week.
Receptionist:	Wednesday 6th at 7.20 a.m. So you'll need the taxi at … <u>3.30</u>. OK. Can I have your name please?
Sam:	Sam Williams.
Receptionist:	And your address?
Sam:	<u>60</u>, Willowside Bank, <u>Abingdon</u>. That's A-B-I-N-G-D-O-N.

Receptionist:	Thank you. And the postcode is?
Sam:	OX14 3HB.
Receptionist:	OX14 3HB. And can I have a contact number for you?
Sam:	Yes, of course. My mobile is 07789 612744.
Receptionist:	Thank you. 07789 612744. Now … we'll be picking you up at 3.30. Is that OK?
Sam:	Yes, that's fine.

Track 08

Flight attendant:	Have you filled in your landing card?
Hua Fang:	No, sorry I'm afraid not. I'm having a few problems.
Flight attendant:	Can I help you at all? little
Hua Fang:	Oh, yes please.
Flight attendant:	Well, the first question's very easy. What's your family name?
Hua Fang:	My family name is Liu, L- I- U.
Flight attendant:	And your first name?
Hua Fang:	Well, my English name is Grace, but my Chinese name is Hua Fang. Which one should I put here?
Flight attendant:	Which name do you have in your passport?
Hua Fang:	Hua Fang. H-U-A and F-A-N-G.
Flight attendant:	So you should put that one. And your date of birth?
Hua Fang:	Shall I put the day first or the month?
Flight attendant:	See where it says D-D, M-M and Y-Y-Y-Y?
Hua Fang:	Yes. What does that mean?
Flight attendant:	It means date, month and year.
Hua Fang:	Oh OK. So I put seventeen, twelve, nineteen ninety four.
Flight attendant:	17th December 1994?
Hua Fang:	Yes, that's right. And what address is this?
Flight attendant:	That would be where you are staying in the UK.
Hua Fang:	Oh OK. Let me see … 13 Park Road, Brighton, B-R-I-G-H-T-O-N. And the postcode, BN40 4GR.
Flight attendant:	Is there anything else you need help with?
Hua Fang:	No, thank you. I understand the other questions. Thank you very much for your help.

Track 09

Receptionist:	Silver Tulip Hotel. Good afternoon. How can I help you?

Edward:	Ah, yes. Good afternoon. I'd like to book a room for next Friday.
Receptionist:	Certainly, sir. How many nights will you be staying?
Edward:	Just one, please.
Receptionist:	And would you like a single or double room?
Edward:	A double room, please.
Receptionist:	A double room. And would you like twin beds or a king sized bed?
Edward:	A king sized bed, please.
Receptionist:	Let me see. Yes, we do have a double room available for next Friday. Would you like me to book it for you?
Edward:	Yes, please.
Receptionist:	Could I have your name, please?
Edward:	Yes, it's Edward Francis.
Receptionist:	Is that F-R-A-N-C-E-S?
Edward:	No. It's F-R-A-N-C-I-S.
Receptionist:	F-R-A-N-C-I-S?
Edward:	Yes. That's right.
Receptionist:	And your home address please, sir.
Edward:	Yes, it's 23, Cypress Avenue, Cambridge
Receptionist:	Is that C-Y-P-R-U-S?
Edward:	No. C-Y-P-R-E-S-S. Like the tree.
Receptionist:	Oh, I see. And your postcode is?
Edward:	CB3 9NF.
Receptionist:	And it's for just one night?
Edward:	Yes, that's right.
Receptionist:	We can reserve a parking space for you. Are you coming by car?
Edward:	Actually, I'll be taking a taxi from the station.
Receptionist:	That's fine. And one last question: would you like dinner and breakfast?
Edward:	No dinner, thank you. But I'd like breakfast.
Receptionist:	Just breakfast. So, to confirm. You're arriving on Friday 16th April and leaving on Saturday 17th. That's one night in a double room with a king sized bed with breakfast.
Edward:	That's right. Thank you very much.

Track 10

Receptionist:	And could I have your mobile number?
Edward:	Yes. It's 07976 122577, Oh no sorry, it's been changed! It's 07961 121597.
Receptionist:	07961 121597. Thank you. Is there anything else I can help you with?
Edward:	Yes, I'm having dinner with a friend. Could you recommend the best a good restaurant near here?
Receptionist:	That would be the Winston Churchill. It's about a mile from here.

Edward:	Perfect. <u>Could you please make a reservation for 7 p.m.</u> and leave a message with the details for my friend when he arrives?
Receptionist:	Certainly. What is the gentleman's name?
Edward:	<u>Mr Alaoui. That's A L A O U I.</u>
Receptionist:	No problem. We look forward to seeing you next week.
Edward:	Thank you.

Unit 2   Food and cooking

Track 11

Here are the ingredients for our special apple cake.

You need <u>500 grams, that's half a kilo of apples,</u> <u>two hundred and fifty grams of sugar – that's a quarter of a kilo</u> – and <u>330 grams, or a third of a kilo, of flour.</u> You also need <u>200 grams of butter, that's a fifth of a kilo</u> of butter. And finally the milk. You need <u>a fifth of a litre of milk or, if you prefer, that's 200 millilitres.</u>

Track 12

OK everyone, could you all pay attention now? Tomorrow we're going to make a popular Caribbean dish, um … chicken and rice. Recipes vary from country to country, but for the moment I'm going to give you the list of ingredients for the basic recipe and leave you to add the flavours and spices to your own taste. Right, are you ready to write this down? OK… First of all, you need a chicken that weighs about 2 kilos. Then, for four people, you'll need <u>750 grams of uncooked rice.</u> OK? For the sauce, you want <u>½ a kilo of onions</u> … Umm and tomatoes, you'll need <u>450 grams of tomatoes</u> and … ah … and what else? Oh, yes, and green peppers you want <u>¼ kilo of green peppers</u> and, finally, <u>50 millilitres of cooking oil.</u> Have you all got that? Good. See you tomorrow, then. Don't forget to bring your favourite spices.

Track 13

Hi, and welcome to 'Campus Cook-in', our daily TV programme for students who want a bit of variety in their meals. Are you bored with cereal for breakfast? Well, today, we're going to tell you how to make pancakes. They're cheap and quick and very easy to make. You only need flour, milk, sugar, salt, oil and an egg. The full recipe's on the university website – just follow the link. So, here we go …

Before you start, it's important to have the exact quantities, otherwise your pancakes won't cook

properly. So please make sure you weigh everything carefully. Everyone ready? OK. First you put the flour, salt and sugar in a large bowl. Next, you mix the egg, milk and oil in another bowl. Then, slowly add the liquid ingredients to the flour mixture, mixing well until it has a smooth, thick consistency. Make sure you stir all the time.

OK? Now we're ready to cook our pancakes. We start by heating the frying pan and greasing it lightly with a little butter. <u>When the butter's melted, we pour a large spoonful of the pancake mix into the pan</u> and cook it until the edges are brown. <u>At that point, flip the pancake over</u> and cook for a minute or so longer. Finally, put the pancake on a plate and cover it up to keep warm, and make the next one. <u>When all your pancakes are ready, you can serve them up with syrup or sugar and lemon, or even fruit.</u> Delicious! Happy Eating!

Track 14

Good morning, everyone. Today we're going to make Apple and Blackberry Crumble. So, I hope you've all bought your ingredients. Ready? Now, let's get straight on with cooking. First, you <u>peel the apples, and cut them into slices.</u> OK? Don't forget to take the middle out of the apple. Now, put the sliced apples in a pan and <u>cook them with some of the sugar.</u> In about 10 minutes they should be nice and soft. Right? Now, <u>mix the blackberries and apple together</u> and <u>put them into the bottom of a baking dish.</u> That's fine … Now, the next thing to do is <u>rub the flour, sugar and butter together</u> with your fingers until it's in tiny pieces, like breadcrumbs. When it's ready, <u>put it on the top of the apples</u> and <u>bake it all in the oven for 30 minutes.</u>

Track 15

Hello everyone. Welcome to the university. I hope you're settling in and beginning to find your way around. I know a lot of students find it hard to adapt to the food. So I thought I'd tell you about a couple of popular English meals that you might hear about. Well, actually, you might've heard of the first one already… it's really popular … it's fish and chips. <u>Fish and chips are fried in deep fat.</u> So it's actually very greasy and <u>not at all healthy.</u> But it's still very <u>popular, especially on a Friday night.</u> That's when a lot of people get their fish and chips from the 'fish and chip' shop, and take them home to eat. <u>The other traditional meal, which is definitely healthier, is Sunday lunch.</u> In England, Sunday lunch is usually <u>some kind of roast meat with vegetables.</u> <u>Traditionally, families have their Sunday lunch at home,</u> but these days quite a lot of families have Sunday lunch in a restaurant.

Track 16

Good afternoon. Many people in the western world eat the wrong food and they eat far too much of it. So the topic of my lecture today is *healthy eating*. I'll divide my talk into three parts; firstly, I'm going to define what I mean by healthy eating. After that, I'll go on to talk about why people don't eat properly and then I'll finish my lecture with some ideas for improving the situation.

Right … So what do I mean by 'healthy eating'? Well, some people might think it means eating a lot of meat. Ummm… of course, vegetarians wouldn't agree with this. They think eating meat is very unhealthy. Other people think that eating a lot of cabbage is good for you, or a lot of salad. Well, naturally, cabbage, salad and meat can all be part of healthy eating. But, for me, a healthy eating means two things: one is… eating a balanced diet and the other is… eating the right amount of food. In my opinion, a balanced diet means eating a variety of foods, including meat, vegetables, fruit, cereals and dairy foods. Obviously, the amount of food we should eat is more difficult to decide. It depends a lot on how active we are.

Track 17

Now on to my next point … Why do so many people eat badly? Well, let's look first at having a balanced diet. To have a balanced diet you have to plan your meals in advance and then buy the right food… and then take time to cook it properly. But, these days people are so busy working that they don't have time to go shopping, so they end up buying fast food at the last minute. Another reason people don't eat well nowadays is that it's actually cheaper to buy food already prepared in a packet. So, people who haven't got much money, will buy packet food rather than cook something fresh. And a final reason why people don't eat healthily … and that is that they don't know how to. In my opinion, schools don't do nearly enough to educate their pupils in healthy eating habits.

Track 18

And now to my third and last point … What can we do to solve the problem? Well, I think it can be solved by three main groups: families, schools and the government. To start with, parents should make sure their children have a healthy diet. Secondly, a lot of schools have self-service machines, where their pupils can buy soft drinks, crisps, sweets and chocolates. I think schools should change what they sell in these machines. Another thing schools can do is make sure that the food they serve in their canteens is fresh and well balanced. And to finish, I'll briefly mention two of the measures I think the government should take to encourage healthy eating. One is to limit advertising unhealthy food and the other is to spend more money on educating the public about the benefits of a healthy diet. In my next lecture, I'll go into more detail about… [fade]

Unit 3   Presentations

Track 19

1	intro*duce*	intro*duction*	
2	presentation	pre*sent* (v)	pre*sent* (n)
3	sug*gest*	sug*gestion*	
4	pro*ject*	pro*jector*	
5	in*form*	in*formation*	
6	ex*plain*	expla*nation*	

Track 20

Farouk:	So, who's going to do the introduction?
Edward:	Well, I suggest you present the first part, Farouk. You've done a lot of work on this project, after all.
Farouk:	Well, OK. I'll start. But you've got a lot of information, too. I think you should explain the next two slides.

Track 21

Beth:	OK, everyone. The first thing we have to decide is our topic. I mean, what exactly are we going to talk about? We know the course is Art History and the subject is Italian painting, but that's still too big. We have to choose a particular topic. What do you think, Mandy?
Mandy:	I think we should concentrate on a single painter.
Edward:	But, on the other hand, if we discuss more than one artist, it'll be easier to make comparisons and show the differences between them.
Farouk:	That's a good idea, Edward. It'll give us more to discuss.
Mandy:	Right. So the next thing is to decide which artists to look at. I think we should definitely include Michelangelo. You know he painted the ceiling of the Sistine Chapel in Rome. He's very famous … and what about Leonardo

da Vinci. They were both great painters. What do you think Beth?

Beth: They're OK, I suppose. But don't you think everyone else will choose them? How about Botticelli? His painting is very different from the other two.

Farouk: I agree with Beth. Why don't we have Michelangelo and Botticelli?

Edward: I'm happy with that. Everyone else OK with it?

Track 22

Edward: Right, guys. Let's have a look at what we're going to put in the slides. The first slide's going to be the introduction, isn't it? So, I guess it should have a title. How about 'Michelangelo and Botticelli: a comparison'?

Mandy: Yeah… So we've got the title. Don't you think we should make a list of bullet points for each of the slides in the presentation?

Farouk: Oh, yes … definitely. How many slides do we have to do?

Edward: Well, the presentation's ten minutes long, so we should probably have a maximum of six slides … Remember that Beth's already got two slides about Botticelli.

Mandy: Well, why don't we do two slides each … that'd be eight, including the introduction and the conclusion?

Edward: That sounds fair enough. Let's do that. So who's going to do the rest of the slides?

Farouk: I can start off with the introduction. And then, I could do the conclusion and the summary at the end. What do you think?

Mandy: Great. I'd like to talk about Michelangelo's paintings. I've done quite a lot of reading about them.

Edward: Fine. So I could do a couple of slides showing how Michelangelo and Botticelli are similar and how they're different.

Track 23

Beth: We want the presentation to look as if it's been made by a team, don't we, Edward? I think we should have a one design for all the slides. Do you agree?

Edward: Oh, yes, of course. We don't want a different colour for each slide. Shall we design a slide now for the rest of the group to use?

Beth: Yes, let's do that. Let's have a look … This slide has the program icon on the title box. Shall we keep it there?

Edward: No, I don't think so. It hasn't got anything to do with the presentation. Let's take that off.

Beth: Fine. And I think we should keep the blue bullet points. They match the light blue title box. What do you think about putting images in each slide?

Edward: Oh, absolutely. I think we should put at least one image on each slide.

Beth: Good. We're agreed, then. Let's send this slide to the others, shall we?

Track 24

Farouk: OK, everyone. I've put all our slides together so we can see if we're happy with the presentation. I think we need to check that we all agree with the order … there's nothing to decide about my slides, the introduction and the conclusion. Obviously, one of my slides goes at the beginning and the other one at the end. Edward's slide, comparing the two artists, will have to go after Beth's and Mandy's. What we need to decide is which artist should go first, Michelangelo or Botticelli.

Mandy: Well, Michelangelo is more famous than Botticelli, isn't he? I mean everyone's heard of him. Maybe he should go first. What do you think, Beth?

Beth: Umm … I'm not sure that just being famous is a good reason to put him first.

Edward: OK, so isn't it sensible to put the artist who was born earlier first? Who was that? When was Michelangelo born?

Mandy: In 1475.

Edward: And Botticelli?

Beth: In 1445.

Edward: So, let's put Botticelli first, and follow with Michelangelo.

Track 25

Tutor: Good morning everyone. So, you're going to tell me about your presentation. First of all, what's your topic? Did you say you were going to talk about the uses of mobile phones?

Laila:	Err … Not exactly. We're actually going to explain the <u>dangers of using mobile phones.</u>
Tutor:	Ahhh… OK… that sounds interesting. What are you going to discuss exactly?
Anne-Marie:	Well, we've planned to divide the presentation into three sections. <u>We'll have an introduction, explaining why we think it's important to understand the dangers of mobiles.</u> <u>Then on the second slide, we'll have a list of the different types of danger</u> and then on the last slide we're going to suggest ways of staying out of danger when you use a mobile.
Harry:	Yes, we want to start by telling the audience that using a mobile phone can be dangerous and then go into more detail in the next part.
Tutor:	OK … but before you talk about the dangers of mobile phones, <u>I think you should mention the advantages.</u> You could put that in your introduction. It balances up the argument a bit.
Harry:	Oh…. yes, I see what you mean. Right… We'll do that.

Track 26

Tutor:	So, shall we have a look at your presentation? Did you bring it with you?
Anne-Marie:	I've got it here on a memory stick. Can we show you on your computer?
Tutor:	Yes, that's fine. Let's have a look. Mmm … Right, as you say, you're going to add <u>the advantages of using mobile phones to the first slide.</u> Good. Who's going to explain the second slide with all the dangers?
Laila:	That's me. Do you think I've got enough detail?
Tutor:	Yes. I think there's plenty of information, but I think it's all a bit mixed up at the moment. I mean, you've got dangers like getting headaches in the same list as having car accidents and being robbed in the street. They're all different types of danger, aren't they? I think you should divide them into groups. Maybe under separate titles, like <u>Health, Accidents and Security.</u>
Laila:	Oh, right. Yes, thank you. That'll make it much clearer to the audience … Mmm … OK.
Tutor:	Now, in the third slide you can put your

	<u>suggestions</u> for staying away from each of these dangers under separate titles.

Track 27

Tutor:	Have you got any other questions? Harry: Ummm…. yes. The presentation should be for 10 minutes, is that right?
Tutor:	Yes. But ten minutes in total, including three minutes for questions. <u>So you'll only talk for seven minutes.</u>
Anne-Marie:	<u>That's only two minutes each!</u> We won't be able to say much in that time, at all!
Tutor:	That's why you have to plan what you're going to say carefully and make sure you only include the most important information. For instance, you won't have time to give examples. But you could put some images on your slides that show examples, without spending time talking about them.
Laila:	Hey, that's a good idea. And the audience can look at them while we talk.
Tutor:	And another thing … <u>make sure all the slides have the same style.</u> You should get together and agree on one style for the whole presentation.
Harry:	OK, we'll do that too. Thanks a lot for your help.

Review 1

Track 28

A B C D E F G H I J K L M N O P Q R S T U V W X Y Z

Track 29

1   The <u>first</u> thing we have to <u>decide</u> is our <u>topic.</u>
2   So, that's <u>fixed</u> then.
3   I <u>think</u> we should <u>keep</u> the <u>blue</u> <u>bullet</u> <u>points.</u>
4   I've put <u>all</u> our <u>slides</u> <u>together.</u>
5   So, let's put <u>Botticelli</u> <u>first,</u> and <u>follow</u> with <u>Michelangelo.</u>
6   <u>Make</u> <u>sure</u> <u>all</u> the <u>slides</u> have the <u>same</u> <u>style.</u>

Unit 4   Work

Track 30

1   Hi. I'm Adam. I'm your Student Union representative and I'm here to tell you about <u>student societies.</u>

2   Good morning everyone. For the last two weeks, we've been looking at employment opportunities in industry, and in today's lecture I'll be talking about <u>working in a large corporation</u>.

3   Hello. My name's Annie and I'm the university careers officer. Today I'm going to talk about <u>working outdoors</u>.

4   Is everyone ready? OK? Remember last week we discussed work in private industry. Well, this week's talk will cover <u>employment opportunities in institutions of further education</u>.

5   Good afternoon. Thank you for inviting me to talk to you. I'm Angus McDonald. I'm a police officer and my topic today is <u>job satisfaction</u>.

6   Good evening. It's good to see so many people here this cold night. OK … my lecture this evening will be about <u>finding a job</u>.

Track 31

1   Hi. My name's Adam. I'm your Student Union rep. and this evening I'm going to talk about the different <u>clubs</u> you can join here at the university.

2   Hello. Thank you all for coming, today. For the last couple of weeks, we've been discussing how to get a job in private industry, and today's lecture is about working in a small <u>company</u>.

3   Hello. My name's Annie and I'm the university careers officer. I've come in this evening to tell you about jobs that involve spending a lot of time <u>outside</u>.

4   Good evening, everyone. Right… last week we talked about working in private education. Well, this week's talk will cover employment in <u>universities</u>.

5   Good afternoon. Thank you for inviting me to talk to you. I'm Angus McDonald. I'm a police officer and today I'll be talking about job <u>fulfilment</u>.

6   Good evening. Thank you for inviting me to talk to you. My topic for this evening will be how to find <u>employment</u>. I hope you'll find it useful.

Track 32

My name's Alice and I work on a <u>farm</u> in the south east of England. Mostly, we grow fruit, but we also keep <u>chickens</u>, ducks and dairy cows. So, we have to work outside quite a lot, even in the winter, when it's cold and dark. That's the worst part of the job, really. You know, having to go out in the rain and snow to feed the <u>animals</u>. <u>But the summer's totally different. I really enjoy being outdoors</u>, helping the fruit pickers and loading the trucks. We deliver most of our fruit to <u>supermarkets</u>, but we also supply <u>local shops</u> with our milk, eggs and cheese. In fact, we produce so much cheese and fruit that we even sell them directly to <u>the public</u> in our farm shop.

Track 33

I'm Wei Long, but my American friends call me Will. I'm a <u>businessman</u> in California. Before I came to the United States, I studied at a university in China. I graduated in information technology. But when I was young, even before I went to university, I worked in the family business. So my ambition has always been to earn a living through <u>trade</u>. After I graduated, I worked for my father for a few years to get some experience and then I started my own <u>small company</u>. First I set up an office in China, and then I opened another office in California. We sell <u>computer parts</u> from China, because I know a lot of people in the computer industry there. I don't have any salesmen, but I have <u>a receptionist</u> to look after the office while I'm out on sales trips. I like being my own boss … I enjoy being able to make all the <u>decisions</u> myself. I mean, I sell most of my goods to large corporations and I think I'd find it very difficult to work in a <u>big company</u>.

Track 34

My name's Khalidah. I'm a doctor in a busy hospital in London. My job is quite stressful because I work in the Accident and Emergency unit. Our hospital is the only one in the area with an A & E. So, all the urgent cases come to us. <u>Mostly we see people who have been in car crashes or had an accident at home</u>. When people arrive at the unit, I have to see them first. <u>I examine them to find out what's wrong</u> and make sure we give them the right treatment. <u>When we're sure the patients aren't in any serious danger, the nurses put all the information in their personal records and find them a bed if they're staying in hospital, or arrange for them to go home if they don't need to stay.</u>

Track 35

Hello, everyone. Thank you for inviting me to give a talk in this series of employment lectures. I'm here this evening to tell you about my job. I'm going to tell you what I like about it, what I don't like about it and what I hope to do in the future. OK … Well, <u>I'm a police officer. I've been in the police for just over five years</u> and part of my job is to give talks to students about police work. People often ask why I joined the police. So maybe I'll start there …I've always been interested in law and order, so I went to study <u>law</u> at university. But … mmm … when I got there I realized that I was more interested in the <u>practical</u> side of law than the theory. So, I applied to work with the police force in my spare time. Then, as soon as I graduated, I was accepted for <u>training</u>.

Track 36

As you know, our job is to protect the public from criminals and defend the law. So, obviously, the police force has to work every day of the week, day and night. This means we're often at work when everyone else is relaxing with friends and family, and we can't always be around for special occasions, like birthdays and New Year's Eve. On top of that we have a lot of extra work at weekends, especially when there's a football match and the fans are out celebrating. So our working hours are one disadvantage of police work. A lot of the time we have to work with the public to avoid problems, and we get special training for that. But we can't always prevent trouble, so another disadvantage of the job is the danger... I mean, we know that some of the people we have to arrest will attack us.

Track 37

Now for the advantages ... Well, one of the advantages is that police work is well-paid. As I've said, it's a difficult job, and police officers work hard for their pay. But there are many more advantages ... for example sometimes the work's fun, especially when we have to protect famous people from their own fans! I've met quite a lot of celebrities in my job and I must say I enjoy seeing them close up and finding out what they're really like as people. But, for me the biggest advantage is the job satisfaction. Speaking for myself, would say I get the most job satisfaction when I help someone or solve a problem in a community. And in the future, I'd like to train to be a detective. I think I'd be good at that.

Unit 5 On campus services

Track 38

1

Max:	Hey, Tony. Where are you going?
Tony:	I'm just going over to the Sports Centre.
Max:	Oh really? I've never been there. Where is it?
Tony:	Oh, It's not far. Go down the path on the left and the Sports Centre is on the other side of the wood.

2

Kate:	Umm ..., excuse me, Suzy. Could you help me?
Suzy:	Yes, of course. What is it?
Kate:	I've got a lecture in the Law School next. Could you tell me where the lecture theatre is?
Suzy:	Oh yes. That's easy. The Law lecture theatre's on the first floor.

3

Kate:	It's a lovely campus, isn't it? The lake's so pretty. What's that building on the other side?
Tony:	Oh, that's the Business School.
Kate:	So, how do you get there?
Tony:	You just follow the footpath round the lake.

4

Max:	Hi, Suzy. Are you going to the theatre, by any chance?
Suzy:	Well, I'm not going there. But I can tell you where it is. Look over there ... that's the theatre, just across the green.
Max:	Oh, OK. Thanks a lot. See you later.

5

Kate:	Errr... Tony, I have got to go in to the city centre. Where can I get the bus?
Tony:	Well, the nearest bus stop is just across the road from the Student Union building.

6

Kate:	Hey, Suzy! Can you tell me where the bank is? I want to get some cash out. I've just realized I still owe you £10.
Suzy:	Oh, OK. Go along to the end of the path until you get to the shop on the corner. Turn left and the bank's right next door.

Track 39

Tom:	Hey, Sandra, how's it going? What do you think of the campus?
Sandra:	I think it's all fantastic. Have you been to the coffee shop in the library, yet?
Tom:	No, I haven't. Where is it?
Sandra:	It's on the ground floor. You know, you can have a break without actually leaving the library. It's really great to meet your friends there.
Tom:	Yeah. That's an excellent idea. And it means you've got somewhere to chat without upsetting people who want to study. I can't concentrate when other people are talking. I usually go upstairs to work in the silent zone, on the fourth floor.
Sandra:	Oh, do you? Is it difficult to study at home, then? Where do you live?
Tom:	I'm living in a hall of residence on campus.
Sandra:	Oh, right. It must be tough trying to study in your room.

Tom: Yeah … It's pretty noisy, especially at the weekends. Are you living on campus, too?

Sandra: Yes. I'm on campus, but there are only four people our house. So it tends to be a bit quieter. It's at the end of the footpath, not far from the Sports Centre.

Tom: Oh, right. I know where you mean. I play football on the pitch next to the Sports Centre. I spend quite a lot of time around there.

Sandra: Well, next time you're in that part, let me know. You can come round for coffee.

Track 40

Vicky: Hello, are you new? I haven't seen you around before.

Pedro: Hi, yeah, yeah … I just arrived. To tell you the truth, I'm a bit lost. I saw on the university website that there are lots of the different food outlets on campus. But I don't know where to find them.

Vicky: Oh, no problem. I can tell you all about them. There really are lots of places to eat on campus. To start with, there's the old college dining room. You can have hot meals three times a day, there. If you want to start the day with a hot breakfast, that's the place to go.

Pedro: OK. So whereabouts is it?

Vicky: It's next to the theatre, just between the bus stop and the shops. But, if you're more into fast food, like burgers … or … umm …Chinese stir-fry, or fried chicken, there's a huge fast food hall in the middle of the campus.

Pedro: Is that the big building between the students' union building and the shops?

Vicky: Yeah … that's right. It's a great place to meet your friends. There's always music and plenty of chat.

Pedro: Sounds like my kind of place!

Vicky: But if you just want a quiet place to have a coffee and a pastry, there's a snack bar by the lake. It has wi-fi and an internet café, and … it has a spectacular view over the lake.

Pedro: Well, thank you very much. Can I invite you … [fade]

Track 41

Chen: Excuse me, Lily. Could you help me? You know we've got an essay to write about eating customs across the world?

Lily: Yeah. We have to borrow some books, don't we?

Chen: Yes, but I missed the library training. Do you think you could show me how to find the books and how to take them out?

Lily: Sure, no problem. Shall I tell you about the different parts of the library, first?

Chen: Oh yes …Thank you very much.

Lily: OK, then, let's look at the plan of the library. Here, you can see the main door in the north that leads into the lobby. In the middle of the building, there's a big open PC zone. The lift and stairs are on the left as you go in, and on the other side of the building there's the library café. That part of the library is pretty sociable … It's a good place to study with friends.

Chen: I really prefer to study alone. Is there anywhere in the library I can go?

Lily: Oh, if you like studying in a quiet place, it's better to go upstairs, to the silent zone. As you come out of the lift, or up the stairs, you'll see a section on your right, facing north, which is closed off. That's the silent zone. On the other side, facing south, are the bookshelves with all the cookbooks … [fade]

Track 42

Chen: Now can you show me how to find a book?

Lily: Well, the library's very big, and the books on food could be under cookery, or they could be in history, or even entertainment. So, the first thing to do is to look the book up in the online catalogue.

Chen: Where do I do that?

Lily: It's easy … there are lots of computers in the library for that.

Chen: OK, I see.

Lily: Right, you look up the title first. When you've found the book, you'll see it has a *class mark* next to it. The class mark is one or two letters and a number … Make a note of the class mark … then look it up on the plan of the library. The plan shows you exactly what section of the library the books are actually kept in.

Track 43

Chen: Thank you very much, Lily. So how do I borrow a book?

Lily: That's simple, too. When you go to the library you'll have to take your student ID card. When want to borrow a book, you take it downstairs to the scanner. Then, scan your ID card first. Then, open the book and slide it under the scanner until it makes a sound… a short beep. And that's all you have to do … Oh, sorry, I forgot. At the end the system prints out a ticket. It's a good idea to keep it for a while, just in case you have a problem with your loan.

Chen: Thanks again, Lily. You've been really kind … [fades out]

Unit 6 Staying safe

Track 44

And now for some local news … When the receptionist arrived at Goodmead Primary school on Monday, she found that someone had broken into the office and stolen several laptops, so she called the police. They came to look at the crime scene straight away and advised her to make sure she locked up the office every evening in future. They also suggested that she should watch out for any strangers nearby. Two days later, the police called to say that they had caught the thieves and arrested them. They said they would take them to court in the next few days.

Track 45

When the receptionist arrived at Goodmead Primary School on Monday, she found that someone had broken into the office and stolen several laptops, so she called the police.

Track 46

Good morning. Thank you for inviting me to talk to you today. I like speaking to students, especially when there's a chance of making their lives a bit safer. Just to start, does anyone know what the most common crime is? No? Well, theft is the most common crime in the UK. There are various kinds of theft. For instance, robbery, when a thief takes something away from someone personally. Like, when you're walking in the street and someone grabs your handbag or your mobile and runs away. That's robbery. Another form of theft is burglary, when a thief breaks into your house and steals your property.

OK. Now I'd like to go on to talk about safety on holiday. You probably know that when you're on holiday abroad, you're in much more danger of being robbed. This is because you probably don't know the country very well. For example you might not realize that you're

in a dangerous area. One of the things you can do to protect yourself is to keep your passport and money in the safe in the hotel. You can always go back and get them if you need them. Another thing you can do is take an old mobile with you on holiday. These new smart phones are very popular with thieves all over the world. It's safer just to take an old one.

Track 47

Hello, everyone. I'm Jennifer and I work for campus security. Welcome to this very short talk about emergency phone numbers. To start with, you need to know that emergency numbers aren't the same in every country. As we're in England at the moment, it's important to know that the emergency number is 999. So you'll need to remember this. Those of you who've been to the United States, will know that the emergency number is 911, one number different. But in Australia, the emergency number is completely different. It's 000.

In Germany, the emergency number is the same as the rest of Europe. That's 112. And in case anyone's thinking of going on holiday to India this summer, it's useful to know that the emergency number there is 100.

Track 48

Good morning. I'm here today to give you a few tips about security on campus. We're not just here to prevent crime, but to make sure you're safe twenty four hours a day.

One of the services we provide for students who live on campus is to walk home with you if you need to cross the campus late at night. I mean, we all know the halls of residence are quite a long way from the library, don't we? So, for example, if you've been studying in the library 'til late and you're nervous about going home alone, all you have to do is ring campus security on 3333 and we'll send someone to make sure you're safe. OK?

By the way, another important thing to remember is the campus emergency number. Umm … we all know the national emergency number in the UK is 999. But when you're on campus … and there's an emergency, you should call 3333. If you call 3333, you'll get through to our own staff, right here on campus. They can react quickly and get to you faster than national services.

Track 49

Good evening, everyone. It's great to be here to talk to you about staying safe on holiday. Before I came this evening, I did a little research on where students like to go for their holidays and came up with two continents: Latin America and India. So, mmm … I've been looking at the crime figures for both areas, and

I thought I'd start by talking a bit about that. Then I'll give you some advice about how to avoid becoming a victim of crime.

OK, first of all, let's look at what kinds of crime are committed most in different continents … Ummm, OK, I'll start with <u>India</u>. Generally, India isn't thought of as a dangerous place for individuals, but there has been an increase in <u>handbag theft</u> in recent years … So keep an eye on your bag when you're out in the street. Right. Now let's look at <u>Latin America.</u> Mmmm … Of course, you do realize that not all Latin American countries are the same, but it is true to say that guns are used in a high percentage of crimes across the continent. Looking at the figures, it seems that <u>gun crime</u> is a serious problem throughout.

Track 50

I can see some of you are thinking that it all sounds rather dangerous. But I know lots of people who've been there and had a really great time. They followed advice from the authorities, like making sure they didn't wear <u>expensive jewellery</u> in the street. And I'd certainly advise anyone travelling to Latin America to do the same. Another thing you should be careful of, is not to go to <u>lonely places</u> at night. But, of course, that's the same anywhere. But I must say , you do have to be very careful in some parts of Latin America when you take your money out of a cash machine. Sometimes, you find that thieves stand very close to people <u>at cash machines</u> and take their money as it comes out.

Track 51

OK … So, now, I'll finish by talking a little bit about India. I've actually been to India and <u>I didn't have any feeling that it was dangerous at all</u>. First of all, I went on an organized tour with a group of people. This is definitely the best way to go because <u>it's so much safer.</u> I mean, I didn't go anywhere without the group, and we had a tour guide who spoke the local language and knew the area. In fact, I remember now, <u>she warned us not to go off with strangers,</u> even if they seemed nice and friendly. But, again, you wouldn't do that at home either, would you?

Unit 7 Studying, exams and revision

Track 52

| Carl: | Hi, Martha, how's the essay going? |
| Martha: | Oh, hi Carl. The essay, oh, you know, there's a lot of reading. It's difficult to |

remember all the different ideas and the different writers.

Carl:	So, how do you keep up with it all?
Martha:	Well, actually, <u>I make a note of the writer's name and summarize their ideas in a note book.</u> It's very old fashioned, isn't it?
Carl:	It is a bit. Actually, I'm quite the opposite. <u>I've downloaded some free software from the internet. It lets me save all the articles and ebooks I get online and make notes on them.</u> I like it because it's cheaper than printing everything. But, what do you do, Enrique?
Enrique:	Oh, I'm afraid my note-taking system isn't as modern as that. And it's much more expensive. <u>I print the articles I find online, and I photocopy pages out of text books. Then I go through and highlight</u> all the important information with a pen. Not very good for the environment, I'm afraid … What about you, Jenny?
Jenny:	Ummm … I'm in the middle, really. I don't use special software, but <u>I keep all the articles I read online in folders on my PC and make notes on them there.</u>

Track 53

Chen:	Hey, Lesley. Are you ready for the exam?
Lesley:	Hi, Chen! I haven't seen you for weeks, Am I ready? I don't know … I've been revising really hard, but I can't remember anything at the moment. You know, I get ready for exams by planning <u>a revision timetable</u>. It helps me make sure I've studied everything on time. But just before an exam, my mind goes blank!
Chen:	Yes, I know what you mean. I've been trying out a new technique for remembering facts and details. I heard about it in a psychology lecture. What you do is <u>put together pictures in your mind of the different things you want to remember.</u> It's usually better if you can make the pictures funny, like cartoons.
Lesley:	I hadn't heard of that. It sounds like fun. Do you do that, too, Indira?
Indira:	Well, I tried it once, but it didn't help me much. I remember things by hearing them in my head. I can't really study in the library when people are

	talking, 'cos I have to be able to hear myself saying things over in my mind! It's easier for me to concentrate if I study at home, late at night, when it's quieter. What do you do to remember things for exams, Mark?
Mark:	Mmmm … I go to bed early the night before the exam and get up very early in the morning, like five o'clock and then I read over my notes again just to refresh my memory. I know a lot of lecturers tell us not to do last minute revision, but it works well for me.

Track 54

Student:	Excuse me.
Receptionist:	Yes?
Student:	Can I take my phone into the exam, if I switch it off?
Receptionist:	Your mobile? No. No mobiles are allowed in the exam hall. You can put it in your bag, though.
Student:	OK, but then what do I do with my bag?
Receptionist:	Bags go in the lockers, down the corridor on the left. There are keys in the doors. Just lock the door and take the key with you. Over here, look, have a look at the poster. When you've put your things away, go to the main door of the exam hall and show the supervisor your student identity card.
Student:	Oh, OK. I see so, I show my identity card at the door and then when I get into the exam hall, I need to look for my examination number. Is that the same number as my identity card?
Receptionist:	Yes, that's right … the same number.
Student:	So where should I look for it?
Receptionist:	Your examination number will be on a desk.
Student:	Ahh.. right. Thank you very much.
Receptionist:	No problem. Good luck.

Track 55

Mac:	Hi guys. Is everyone set to study for the exams, then? Does anyone have any hints about how to get ready for them? I'm not sure where to start, really. Any ideas, Barbara?
Barbara:	Well, Mac … there are lots of things we could do. I mean we could start by looking at old exam papers, or we could go through all the lecture notes for each subject. What do you think?

Mac:	I think it's better to go through this year's lecture notes first. I mean, the exam topics might have changed since last year. Do you agree, Gerry?
Gerry:	Yeah. I think you're right. The lecture notes will tell us what the main topics of the subject are. Do you think we could ask the tutors what the exam topics might be?
Mac:	I think we could ask and they might tell us roughly what to look at, but I don't think they'll tell us exactly what the topics will be.
Barbara:	I think it's a good idea to ask them, just to know what to focus on. So what's next? What do you think about reading all the books on the reading list? Gerry?
Gerry:	Ahhh … I don't think that's a very good idea. … we can't read all the books.
Barbara:	I think you're right. What I think we have to do is try to remember the most important details and arguments from the main writers and be ready to use them in the exam.
Mac:	Yeah. OK. Then the next thing to do is look at old exam papers and see what kind of questions we might get.
Gerry:	Yes. That's where the old exams will help … looking at the type of question.
Mac:	Right. So when we've worked out which topics we need to study and remembered the main ideas, we can look at old papers and write a few practice questions.
Barbara:	Yes. And that'll help us [fades out]

CD 2

Track 01

Tutor:	Morning, everyone. I thought we'd get together today and just talk about exam techniques. I'm sure everyone has different ideas about them. So shall we find out what you do first when you get into an exam?
Gerry:	Check that you have the right exam paper?
Tutor:	It sounds funny, but students do actually answer the wrong exam paper sometimes! So, check that it's your exam, first. Then what?
Gerry:	Write your examination number on the answer sheet?
Tutor:	Well, it might sound obvious, but writing your examination number at

the beginning of the exam can be a good idea. Apart from making sure the examiner knows who wrote the exam, can anyone say why?

Mac: It can help you relax.

Tutor: Yes, that's right. Doing something easy like that gives you a chance to calm down. Right, so what do you do next?

Barbara: Read the questions carefully?

Tutor: Well, before you read the questions, what should you do?

Mac: Read the instructions.

Tutor: Yes. You should read the instructions next. You need to know how many questions you have to answer, and whether you have to answer all the questions, or only some. What other important information do you need to check before you start?

Gerry: How much time you have?

Tutor: Yes, Gerry's right. You need to make sure that you know how long the exam is, so you can manage your time properly.

Track 02

Tutor: OK. What do you do next?

Barbara: Read the questions?

Tutor: Yes. It's very important to read the questions. Not just once, but several times.

Mac: I usually make a few notes when I'm looking at the questions. Sometimes a question looks easy and then when you start writing you realize that it's actually more difficult than you thought.

Gerry: Yeah, but you don't want to spend too much time writing notes.

Tutor: No … but it's a good idea to jot down a few ideas to see if you can remember the arguments for the topics you studied most.

Barbara: Once we've decided, is it better just to start at the beginning and answer the questions as they appear on the exam? Or should we start with the easy questions?

Gerry: Mmmm. Well, I start with the questions that I know better. And leave the ones I'm not sure of for the end.

Mac: That's what I do, but I still keep an eye on the clock, especially, when the questions are all worth the same number of marks,

Track 03

Tutor: Mac's right. If you write one very good answer, but it's only worth thirty per cent of the marks, you still lose the other seventy per cent on that exam.

Gerry: So, it's better to write our main ideas for a question even if we don't have time to answer it properly.

Tutor: Yes, absolutely. We can't give you marks for writing nothing. But, if you give us your main ideas, we can give you some marks.

Barbara: Oh, really! I wish I'd known that in my last exam. I spent all my time writing a long answer to one of the questions and didn't get round to the other two. I didn't understand why I got such a low mark.

Mac: Yeah. That's what happened to me. Luckily, my tutor explained it afterwards and I never did it again.

Unit 8   Shopping and spending

Track 04

1. I bought this shirt in a sale.
2. My brother thinks online shopping is much quicker than going to the shops.
3. The good thing about shopping in a department store is that you can get everything in one place.
4. The last time I took something back to a shop, the customer services manager wasn't there.
5. I lost my credit card the other day. I was really worried someone else would use it.
6. Have you ever bought a train ticket with a student discount? It's so much cheaper.

Track 05

Interviewer: Could you tell me something about who does the shopping in your family?

Miriam: Of course. Well, in a way, it depends on what kind of shopping you mean. There are four people in my family but only two of us actually go shopping. I think we're like most families, really. I mean, my mother always buys the food. She's very organized, you know, she always makes a shopping list before she goes out. She says it's a good way to save money. Anyway, she goes to the supermarket once a week and gets everything we need. My father and brother hardly ever go to the shops, but I love shopping! I'm the person in our family who goes shopping the most. I just love to go to the shopping mall with my friends. Sometimes, I buy clothes on the spur of the moment, you know, without planning to. But quite often, when I get home I don't really like what I've bought and I have to go back and ask for a refund. I don't like doing that very much. I think it's a bit embarrassing.

Track 06

Hi. This is our last lecture about business and advertising this term and today I'm going to talk about shopping habits in different parts of the world. First we'll look at who normally does the shopping. Yes, umm .... Well, in the United Kingdom about 75% of the food shopping is done by women. But this isn't the case everywhere. There are countries where up to 60% of men do the grocery shopping on their way back from work. And, habits are changing … even in western countries … for example, a recent survey showed that in the United States nearly 50% of men shop for groceries.

Now let's look at where people shop. In fact, where people shop depends on whether they live in the city or in the country. As we all know, there are more supermarkets in the city and more markets and small shops in the country. So as the population moves to the city to find work, more people are shopping in supermarkets than ever before … [fades out]

Track 07

Hello. Good to see you all here. This afternoon I'm going to talk about a recent survey into men's and women's shopping habits. Before I start, I'd like you to look at the list of statements about men and women and see which ones you would expect to be true … Right? Firstly, let's look at the idea that women spend a lot of money on expensive shoes. Actually, this isn't true. In fact, women buy a lot of cheap shoes. Men, on the other hand, try to save money by buying special offers. What is surprising about women, though, is that they like shopping in expensive boutiques. And, it isn't true that they always make a shopping list when they go to the supermarket. We also expected to find that men would go to the supermarket after midnight to get their food cheaper, but this wasn't the case, either. Then the third thing we learnt about women is that they like to shop in big department stores, which men don't like. They like to go shopping in specialist shops. OK? How many did you get right?

Track 08

Good evening everyone. This evening, I'm going continue last week's lecture by talking more about how people spend their money. First of all, I'm going to compare how people of different age groups spend their cash. You probably know that there's a lot of difference between what young people do with their money, how families spend their money and what more mature people do. Secondly, I want us to think about what we imagine men and women spend their money on. And then, I'm going to look at male and female spending patterns and see whether we were right.

OK … To start with, let's divide the population into three sections: let's say, ahhh, young people up to the age of 30 in the first group. Then … ummm … let's put families in the 30 to 55 year old group. So that puts adults over 55 in the mature group. Does that make sense?

Track 09

Right, well, I found that the first group, that's young people up to the age of 30, mostly spend their money on clothes, music and entertainment. That's not really very surprising, is it? Although I must admit I thought they might spend a lot on cars and travelling around. So … the next group is what I've called *families*, people in the age group from 30 to 55. Naturally, as I expected, this group spends most of its money on food, toys and trips out. But, I was surprised to find that people aged between 30 and 55 spend most of their money on furniture and kitchen equipment. I suppose it's logical, if you think about it. People are usually improving their homes at that age and household equipment is very expensive. But they also spend a lot of money on electronic equipment, like video games for the children. Now turning to the third group, that's people over 55 … I thought they'd spend their money on gardening tools and electronic equipment. But I was wrong again. People in the over 55s group spend most money on new cars and days out.

Track 10

So, what did we think about how men and women spend their money? OK … Well, we thought that young women would spend a lot on clothes and shoes, and that young men would buy more electronic equipment and cars. Well, when we look at the figures we can see that we were right about the men. Young men spend twice as much as women on cars and computers. But … and this is interesting … we were wrong about the women. I was surprised to find that young women spend much more on beauty treatments than they do on clothes and shoes. So we'll have to think about that again. And there's another interesting fact about young women … It looks as though young women are much more concerned about their diet than men. We found that although young women don't spend as much as men on eating out, they do spend a lot more on organic foods than young men.

Unit 9 Hobbies, interests and sports

Track 11

A

Karl: Hi Trudy. What are you doing this weekend? I'm going swimming, down at the beach.

Trudy: Oh, right … I'm going running. I'm practising for the marathon next month. Do you like running, Karl?

Karl: No. Not me!

B

Hillary: Hey, Karl, do you feel like going to the cinema tonight? There's a really good film on.

Karl: Oh, I'm sorry Tracey. I've already got tickets to go a concert this evening.

C

Trudy: What are you doing this vacation, John? I'm travelling around Europe for a while before I go back to Australia.

John: Oh, really? I'm not that keen on travelling, to be honest. I'm going to spend my vacation gardening.

D

Trudy: I'm going cycling on Saturday, Hillary. Do you want to come along?

Hillary: Thanks a lot, but I've got a lot of cooking to do for the party in the evening. I hope you're still coming.

Trudy: Of course I am. Wouldn't miss it!

Track 12

1 fry fry
2 pray pray
3 lead lead
4 blade blade
5 correct correct
6 play play
7 read read
8 fly fly
9 played played
10 collect collect

Track 13

Martin: So, Sally, what do you do in your free time?

Sally: Well, at the moment I'm training to be a private pilot.

Martin: No way! Really? What made you want to do that?

Sally: Well, I've always loved the idea of flying a plane, ever since I was a little girl.

Martin: Wow! Isn't it expensive?

Sally: Err …, yeah, but it's worth it … It's an amazing experience. But what about you, Martin? What do *you* do for leisure?

Martin: Nothing nearly as exciting … I play ice hockey in my spare time. I'm captain of the college team. So at weekends, we travel to games all over the state.

Sally: But that sounds fun. Do you enjoy leading the team?

Martin: Yeah, I do.

Track 14

Judy: Hi, Steve. What are you doing?

Steve: Well, I collect stamps with pictures of tropical birds on them. So, I'm looking for more of those.

Judy: Oh … that's interesting. Which ones have you got so far?

Steve: I've got a 32 cent stamp with a picture of a *cardinal honeyeater* on it. It came out in 1998.

Judy: A *cardinal honeyeater*? Is that a bird? Can I see?

Steve: Yeah, here … It's a tropical bird.

Judy: Oh, yes. It's beautiful … So which country is the stamp from?

Steve: The United States.

Judy: Mmmm … and how did you get it? Do you know someone in the States?

Steve: No. It's not like that. I buy stamps from other collectors. Look at this one … I bought it last week. It's a twenty five cent stamp.

Judy: Oh, brilliant! It's got a parrot on it! When was it issued?

Steve: 1967

Judy: OK … And where's it from?

Steve: It's from Brazil.

Judy: Cool!

Track 15

Administrator: Hi, can I help you? Are you interested in climbing, at all?

Andrew:	Hi. Yeah. Actually, I've been thinking about joining a club for a while now. So what do I have to do?
Administrator:	It's easy really. I can fill in the form for you right now, online, and then you can come to our first meeting next month.
Andrew:	OK. Let's do that then.
Administrator:	Right. First of all, what's your name?
Andrew:	Andrew.
Administrator:	Andrew … and your family name?
Andrew:	Metcalfe.
Administrator:	Metcalfe … How do you spell that?
Andrew:	M-E-T-C-A-L-F-E
Administrator:	M-E-T-C-A-L-F-E, with an 'e'.
Andrew:	Yes, that's right
Administrator:	And your age? Are you over 18?
Andrew:	Yup. I'm 21
Administrator:	And where do you live?
Andrew:	My address is 43A Highbury Square, London, W1
Administrator:	Thanks … and do you have a number where I can contact you?
Andrew:	Yes, my mobile is 07209 571324
Administrator:	And I have to ask a couple more questions. Ummm … do you have any health problems?
Andrew:	No, no. Nothing.
Administrator:	And a last question. Have you ever climbed before?
Andrew:	Yes, I have, a bit.
Administrator:	Well, thanks very much.

Track 16

Victoria:	Hello. Are you the person to ask about joining a club?
Mark:	Yes, I am. What would you like to know?
Victoria:	Well, I'm interested in several things, but I'd like to know more about the different clubs and how much they cost. I'm looking for a small club that's not too expensive.
Mark:	OK. Have a look at this table. You can see the names of the clubs, the fees and the number of members. I'm afraid they aren't in any order. If you look at the top of the list, the first club is table tennis. That's one of our new clubs.
Victoria:	Oh, right. So the table tennis club costs £20. That's quite expensive.
Mark:	Yes, it is a bit expensive. The cross country cycling club is cheaper, though. Membership fees are only £15, but on the other hand it's got 100 members.

Victoria:	The film and drama club costs a lot, doesn't it?
Mark:	Yes, £50 is a lot. And that's probably why it only has 12 members. Ahhh … is there any other club you think looks interesting? Look at the next one … street dance. Have you ever done any street dance?
Victoria:	No, I haven't, really.
Mark:	It's the cheapest. It only costs £5.
Victoria:	Mmmm …

Track 17

Mark:	OK. Shall we start with your interests? What do you like doing best?
Victoria:	Ummm … well, I like photography. I've got a professional camera. So I take it quite seriously. But I can't really imagine belonging to a club to take photographs. I usually go on long walks on my own and take photos. So I like photography, but I wouldn't want to join a club to do it.
Mark:	OK, so what else do you like doing? Running?
Victoria:	Oh no! Not running! I like walking, but I hate running. I'm afraid the running club isn't for me or the cycling club.
Mark:	And film and drama?
Victoria:	Ahh, no … It's far too expensive. But I do like yoga. I've practised yoga on and off for years. How many members does the yoga club have?
Mark:	It's always a small group. A lot of people sign up at the beginning of term, but they stop going after a few weeks. So they're left with a few regular members every year.
Victoria:	That sounds good. I think I'd like to join the yoga club. And what about the contemporary dance club? Is it expensive?
Mark:	Contemporary dance? No, it's not expensive. £10 for the term … Do you like dance?
Victoria:	Well, I've never tried contemporary dance, but I do like jazz and tap dance. How often does the group meet?

Track 18

Mark:	So can I have your full name, please?
Victoria:	Victoria Mandeville.
Mark:	M-A-N-D-A-V-I-L
Victoria:	No, no. M-A-N-D-E-V-I-L-L-E.
Mark:	Double L, E. Thank you. And how old are you?

Victoria:	Nineteen.
Mark:	And your address?
Victoria:	57 Bury Gardens, Atherton Park, Manchester, M46
Mark:	How do you spell 'Bury'? B-E-R-R-Y?
Victoria:	No. It's B-U-R-Y
Mark:	Right. B-U-R-Y. And do you have a contact number?
Victoria:	Yes. My mobile is: 07942 573 279
Mark:	07942 573 279?
Victoria:	Yes, that's right. Is that all?
Mark:	Ahh … one more thing. Do you have an email address?

Review 3

Track 19

1   … we thought that young women would spend a lot on clothes and shoes, and that young men would buy more video games, mobile phones and cars.

2   We found that although young women don't spend as much as men on eating out, they do spend a lot more on organic foods than young men.

3   … in fact, people aged between 30 and 35 spend most of their money on furniture and kitchen equipment … People are usually improving their homes at that age and household equipment is very expensive.

Unit 10   Work-life balance

Track 20

Their holidays start at the beginning of July.
Listen again.
Their holidays start at the beginning of July.

Track 21

When you start university you'll probably find it's not all that easy to balance the time you spend on studying with the time you spend going out with your friends. In fact, one of the biggest problems you'll have is managing your time. Of course, it's perfectly understandable … I mean, in many cases, it's probably the first time you'll have lived away from home. So you'll have to do lots more things for yourself, like buying your own food, washing your clothes and managing your own money. At the same time, there's no-one there to tell you what time to come home at night, or what time to get up in the morning. On top of that, at university you won't have as many hours of class as you did at school, and your tutors will expect you to study on your own a lot more. So you might feel you've got a lot of free time on your hands. So how do you deal with it? Well, to be honest, I don't think there's an easy answer, but I think it helps to go to all your classes, however tired you are. Print a copy of your timetable and put it on the wall in your bedroom. Actually, your university might even have a system for alerting you on your mobile when your lectures are. Apart from that, you could try not going out during the week and keeping your social life for the weekend. I'm not sure that's very easy though. One thing I will say, though, is that at the end of the year, after your exams, you can really relax.

Track 22

I started this new job a couple of weeks ago and I'm having a lot of trouble with my work-life balance. In my last job we had fixed hours. We had to be at the office at 9.00 on the dot and we always finished at exactly 5.00. Any work we hadn't finished we could just leave for the next day. But this new job's very different. I mean, in this job, we can come into the office any time between 8.00 and 10.00 in the morning. Then we can choose whether to have a lunch break or not. Then it gets a bit complicated … Ummm … If we have a lunch break we can leave between 4.00 and 6.00. If we don't have a lunch break, we can go home between 3.00 and 5.00. OK, well at first this system sounded really good, especially for me because I have young children. But, the problem is that, if we haven't finished our work, we have to finish it off at home. So it's actually very difficult to draw the line between work and home. For example, on Mondays I can leave the children at school, go to the gym and get into the office quite late. But I can't take a lunch break, because I need to leave early to pick the children up from school. They come out at 4.00. And then I have to work from home in the evening to finish what I have to do.

Track 23

If you look at this chart you can see how we plan our projects. This one is a survey we're working on this year about where people liked to shop. OK? Well, we always start by having a team meeting. That's in the first column called tasks. So, in this team meeting we decide what we need to do, who's going to do it and … err … when it's got to be ready. Right? So you can see here in the second column, we've got the start date of the project. That's the 23rd January. That's the same day we have the team meeting. If you look down the tasks column you can see that the first thing we have to do is write a draft questionnaire. You know, like an outline of the questions we want to ask. Then we have to check the questionnaire to make sure the questions are right. If you look at the lines in column three, you can see the dates when we have to complete important tasks in the project. These are what we call milestones in the project. For example, when we've checked the questionnaire on the 25th April, we'll have reached a milestone, and when we've completed the survey on the 30th June, we'll have reached another milestone. On the 15th August, when we finish entering the data on the database, when we finish entering the data on the database, we'll have finished the first phase of the project. The second phase of the project involves writing the report. We'll be doing that between 15th August and the 15th September. And that's the deadline for the project to be handed to the client.

Track 24

In our company we believe that our employees are more productive, you know, they work better, if they're happy. Naturally, we have to make sure the company makes a profit, but at the same time we need to think about the physical and mental health of our employees. We do understand that they aren't just working machines … So we have a policy of helping them find a fair balance between their work and their private lives. What we call a work-life balance. We do this in several ways. Firstly, we have a family friendly policy, so parents can look after their children when they're very young. For example, sometimes they need to work flexible hours, you know, times that aren't fixed. Other times parents have to work part time … and quite a lot work from home. Another example of our family friendly policy is our generous maternity leave package. In our company, we allow women who've had a baby to take a whole year off work after the baby's born. And, of course, while they're away, their jobs are protected.

Track 25

Because we want our employees to be happy, we carried out a survey recently, to find out which working patterns are really most popular. In general, our staff prefer to work at the office. In fact, nearly half come in during regular office hours … you know, from 9.00 to 5.00. Anyway, we also asked about part-time work, working from home and another option … [pause] job sharing. Job sharing is a kind of part-time work, where two people share the responsibilities for one full time job. Anyway, we found that only 5% of our staff wanted to share a job. So, it's not very popular, on the whole. But when it comes to working part-time, we were surprised to find that 27% of our employees would actually prefer it. That's a very high number, really … over a quarter of the staff … And then it was interesting to see that quite a lot of our staff – 20% in fact, would like to work from home.

Track 26

I'd like to give you an example of the kind of person who benefits most from our family friendly policy. Sally is one of our assistants in accounting, who has two small children. Sally's husband travels abroad a lot so she has to look after the children on her own most of the time. Both the children go to a nursery early in the morning. So, we've agreed that Sally can come in at 8 o'clock, after she leaves the children. At lunchtime Sally's sister picks the children up from the nursery. But she has to go to work herself at three o'clock. So Sally leaves the office at two to collect the children from her sister's. And she makes up the extra time by finishing her work at home.

Unit 11   Comparing cultures

Track 27

Conversation A

Sam:	Hey, Mick. Have you ever been to Thailand?
Mick:	Yeah. I was there last year. Why do you ask?
Sam:	Well, I'm thinking of doing a project on Asian food and was wondering whether Thai food was the same as Chinese.
Mick:	Oh, right. Umm … Thai food's not exactly the same as Chinese, but they both have a really healthy diet, with lots of vegetables. Some of the dishes are pretty hot and spicy, though.

Conversation B

Lisa:	Hi, Tony. Do you have a moment?
Tony:	Sure. What's it about?
Lisa:	Well, I'm researching types of housing across the world and I thought I'd ask you about what kinds of houses there are in Australia.
Tony:	Sure. Which part of Australia are you thinking about? I mean, there are blocks of flats in most cities, the same the same as anywhere else in the world.

Conversation C

Li Li:	Hi, Barbara. How's your Japanese language project going?
Barbara:	It's great! I'm learning about the Japanese alphabet at the moment. And what about your project about China? How many languages do they speak?

Li Li;	Ah. Well there's Mandarin Chinese and at least another ten varieties of Chinese from different regions.
Barbara:	Wow! That's amazing!

Conversation D

Debbie:	Amira ... I'm doing a project on national costumes. Do you have one in the Emirates?
Amira:	Oh, yes we do ... The national costume for women is called an abaya. It's basically a long black dress, but we decorate it with gold patterns around the sleeves and neck. It's usually made of a kind of silk. Look at this one, here [pause]. What do you think?
Debbie:	Oh. I think it's lovely.

Track 28

Tony:	I'm trying to find out if people from northern countries have the same attitudes to talking to strangers in public as people from southern countries.
Tutor:	OK. So ... what **have** you found out?
Tony:	Ummm ... Well, I found that in some countries it's more common to talk in public than others. For example, people in the UK and Holland don't usually talk to people they don't know, but the Italians and the Spanish seem to be much more open. They chat to people on buses, in shops, in restaurants.
Tutor:	So, do you think that people from the south of Europe are friendlier than northern Europeans?
Tom:	Well, it does look that way, even in the same country. I mean ... ahhh ... for example, in comparison with Italians from the north of Italy, the Italians in the south chat much more to each other in public.
Tutor:	Mmmm ... it does sound interesting. Well, that's fine. I think you've found a good topic.

Track 29

Meena:	Hi, Barbara. Why don't you join our group? We're going to give a presentation about what we eat at each meal in our home countries.
Barbara:	Oh, great! I love finding out about other cultures. So where do we start? Breakfast? In the UK we have cereal,

toast, eggs and tea or coffee for breakfast. Have you got that, Meena?

Meena:	Yes ... But breakfast in India is completely different. We have a lot of different kinds of breakfast across India, but mostly we eat some type of bread with lentils.
Chen:	Oh, is that right? In China, we have tea with noodles or rice and vegetables for breakfast. So what do you have for lunch, Barbara?
Barbara:	Well, you know in the UK, we don't usually have a big lunch. We usually just have a sandwich. But it's different in India isn't it?
Meena:	Oh definitely. I don't like sandwiches at all. We have rice and vegetables for lunch in India.
Chen:	Yeah ... we have a cooked meal at lunch time, too. We usually have noodle soup, and a main course.
Barbara:	We have our main meal in the evening in the UK, as well. Quite often we have chicken, meat or fish with potatoes and vegetables.

Track 30

Amira:	Hi, Meena. Shall we have a look at the material for our presentation on marriage customs?
Meena:	Yeah, sure. I've got a lot of information about India. How about you?
Amira:	Yes, yes. I've got material about marriage in the Emirates. Shall we get going? What about meeting? How do people in India meet in the first place?
Meena:	Mmm ... in traditional Indian families the parents used to arrange the marriage, and the couple used to meet for the first time when the boy visited the girl's house. But that's changed now.
Amira:	Yeah? We used to have arranged marriages in the Emirates, too. Did the groom have to give anything to the bride's family? I mean, did they give them a gift or money?
Meena:	Well, in India, in the old days, the girl's family used to give the boy's family a gift, like money or jewellery. But, it's not allowed any more.
Amira:	Wow! In my country the groom still has to pay all the expenses! Ummm ... have there been any changes in marriage customs in India in recent years?

Meena:	Well, yes. I've found an article about special websites for finding partners. It says that because so many young people from India study abroad these days, their <u>families are using websites to find marriage partners</u> for them.
Amira:	Oh, OK. And where does the couple live when they get married?
Meena:	That's another thing that's changing. In the past, the bride used to go to live with the family of the groom. But, <u>these days</u>, more and more young couples are setting up their own homes, <u>independently</u>. What about the Emirates?

Track 31

Tutor:	Good morning. Shall we start by looking at the topic of your project? So, what have you decided to research?
Alice:	Well, we thought we'd compare festivals in different countries and see if any of them are similar.
Jack:	Yeah, you know, like the Carnival celebrations in South America and the Water Festival in Thailand.
Tutor:	OK. What exactly are you planning to study? The origins of the festivals? The types of celebration? People's attitudes towards the festivals?
Alice:	We were planning to look at the <u>origins of the festivals</u> and the time of year they're celebrated. We're thinking of looking at the connection between the seasons in different countries and the actual festivals and then looking for similarities between countries that are quite far apart.
Tutor:	Well, that sounds interesting. Did you say you've already started researching into the Carnival?
Jack:	Yes. We've already found a <u>connection between the carnival and the seasons</u>. For instance, some researchers say that a very long time ago, in Europe, people used to put on colourful masks and costumes at the beginning of the year to celebrate the end of winter. And then they could get ready for spring.

Track 32

Tutor:	Right ... and then what happened.
Alice:	Well, as the years went by, the purpose of the carnival changed, and it became a <u>religious festival</u>. These days there are big carnival celebrations

in <u>countries all across the world</u>, like Brazil and India and Indonesia. But an interesting thing we discovered is that in some countries, people celebrate the carnival by throwing water at each other in the street. Well, we thought that, obviously, this is because the carnival's celebrated at <u>the hottest time of the year</u>, just before the rainy season. So, splashing people with water is a very good way of cooling them down.

Track 33

Tutor:	Mmm ... yes, that makes sense. Er ... did you look into any other festivals?
Jack:	Yes, we did! What we're planning to do is more research into <u>water festivals</u>. We found that in Asian countries, where there aren't any carnival celebrations, there are still festivals that involve people splashing each other with water. Actually, we've found references to them in <u>Burma, Thailand, Vietnam, China and Japan</u>. But we also found a reference to a water festival in <u>Mexico</u>. So we thought we'd look into that a bit more and see if we can find any similarities between these countries. Ummm ... I mean, we realized that water is more than just a way of cooling people down in hot weather. It also has a lot of different religious meanings and purposes. For instance, we found that, in some societies, water can mean <u>life</u>, or <u>wealth</u>, or just <u>luck</u>.
Alice:	Yes ... and another thing we found out is that these water festivals often celebrate the beginning of the <u>new year</u>, just like the original celebrations hundreds of years ago before the carnival. So ... umm up to now, we've found that the carnival and the seasons are linked <u>by ancient traditions</u> and that water plays in important part in the celebrations.

Unit 12   Exploring the oceans

Track 34

I'm going to start this lecture by describing the structure of an off-shore oil rig. Well, to be accurate, we should call it an oil platform. If you look at the diagram, you can see the top part of the platform, floating on the surface of the water. The tall tower in the centre of the platform is called a derrick. That's D-E-R-R-I-C-K. The derrick is where the drilling machinery and lifting equipment is installed. OK? Now, if you look about half way down the diagram on the right you can see a helicopter. It's parked on the helicopter pad. Helicopters are used mostly to transport employees to and from the platform when they have free time. Now, if you look underneath that, at the very bottom of the platform you can see one of the four support towers. These support the rest of the platform. These metal structures are usually attached to the sea bed by long cables. Right, now the last part of the platform I'm going to describe is on the other side, just above the level of the water. It's a crane, that's spelt C-R-A-N-E. Cranes are used everywhere in construction, but this one is specialist equipment for lifting heavy spare parts at sea. In fact, apart from the derrick you can see three cranes in the diagram.

Track 35

Some experts believe that if we knew how to control the power of the sea, we could generate enough electricity for the whole world. But, in this talk, I'm going to focus on the UK, and our capacity for generating electricity from wave and tidal energy. I'm going to look at how many megawatts we generated before 2008 and how many we expect to produce in 2014. So, if you'd like to look at the chart, you'll see that before 2008, our capacity was only one megawatt. But in 2008 when oil prices rose, there was an increased interest in marine power and our capacity grew quite dramatically to four megawatts. Ahhh … now, you might have expected this figure to rise consistently over the years, but, in fact it dropped again in 2009 to only two megawatts. This was because oil prices fell again, so there was less interest in developing alternative power sources. But, nowadays the cost of oil production is going up again, and there's been a renewed interest in marine power. As a consequence, capacity has increased steadily since 2009, reaching 18 megawatts in 2012. This trend is expected to continue in the near future, reaching a total capacity of 50 megawatts in 2013 and 60 megawatts in 2014.

Track 36

Good evening. My talk this evening will cover three main themes. First, I'll outline a timeline of how deep sea exploration vessels developed. Secondly, I'll describe the most recent of these, the Deep Sea Challenger, and finally, I'll look at some of the benefits of this deep sea research.

OK. To start with, let's look at how underwater exploration vehicles have developed over the years.

The first manned deep sea exploration vessel was invented in the 1920s. It was called a bathysphere, better known as a Diving Bell. It was basically a round metal structure with windows with just enough room for two men to sit in, and it was lowered into the ocean on a cable. The first descent in the Diving Bell took place in 1930, and in 1934 it went down to a depth of nearly a thousand meters, which was impressive for the time. The problem with the Diving Bell was that it had no power of its own and there wasn't much room for the researchers to move around. So the next development after the Diving Bell was the bathyscaphe, a small manned submarine, invented in the 1940s. The difference between the two was that the bathyscaphe had its own power source which allowed the scientists to investigate in the depths of the ocean more freely. A bathyscaphe called The Trieste reached a record depth of ten thousand meters in 1960. Since then a new record has been set by James Cameron, who descended to a depth of eleven thousand metres for the first time in 2012.

Track 37

So let's move on now to look at the submarine that took James Cameron so far down into the ocean. If you look at the drawing of the Challenger you can see the pilot's chamber at the very bottom of the submarine. It's a very small section where the pilot sits and controls the sub and all the equipment on it. Now let's have a look at how the submarine is powered. Going up from the pilot's chamber, in the middle of the sub, on the right hand side of the drawing, you can see a whole section covered in batteries. They provide the power source that takes the sub all the way to the bottom of the ocean and back up to the surface again. Next to that there's another important part of the sub … Ummm … You probably realize that there's no light at the bottom of the ocean, so the sub needs to take its own. If you look at the back of the sub, in the middle, just next to the batteries, you can see the panel of lights . They provide the light for filming and taking samples from the sea bed. And one more part of the sub, which is important for navigation and to stop it spinning out of control, is the large fin at the back. You can see it at the back of the sub, at the top of the drawing.

Track 38

OK, to conclude my talk, I'm going to ask a couple of questions. First, what is the purpose of this deep sea exploration … and second, is it worth the expense? I think one of the justifications for spending so much money on this kind of research is that it allows scientists to understand more about the surface of the earth, for example how it was formed and how it behaves. This could have important consequences for predicting earthquakes and saving lives through early warning systems. Another reason this type of research is considered valuable is that by exploring unknown parts of the ocean we increase our knowledge of the availability of minerals for industry. And, obviously, this could lead to huge commercial advantages. So the answer is, yes. In the long run this kind of exploration can benefit both the ordinary population and industry.

Review 4

Track 39

1 Abdul studies every evening until 9.00.
2 Thank goodness you're home before dark!
3 Arabic is one of the most difficult languages to learn.
4 Our classes start again in September.
5 In many Asian countries the diet is very healthy.
6 Communication helps people from different cultures to understand each other.

Practice test

Section 1
Questions 1–3
Track 40

Travel Agent:	Hello, Travel Wide, can I help you?
William:	Oh, yes. Good morning. I'm looking for a hotel for a long weekend.
Travel Agent:	OK. First of all, ummm … Where would you like to stay? I mean, are you looking for a peaceful weekend in the country, a busy city break or a relaxing time at the beach?
William:	Well. I certainly want a quiet weekend. I work very hard, so I'd like to relax for a few days.
Travel Agent:	Right … So, it would be country or beach. Which would you prefer?
William:	Mmmm … the beach is very relaxing, but I think I'd rather go to the country this time.
Travel Agent:	OK. That's fine. Let me have a look at country hotels. Would you like to stay at a spa hotel, where you could swim, read, eat healthy food and have

relaxing treatments? Or would you prefer a family hotel on a farm?

William:	Ahh … I must say I like the idea of a spa.
Travel Agent:	Well, that's great! Now, let's just look at our spa hotels. Mmmm … You definitely don't want the beach?
William:	No. I'd like to go somewhere in the countryside. Somewhere where I can go for walks.
Travel Agent:	OK … then it won't be the Ocean Waves Resort. Farmhouse Getaways is a family run hotel in the country, but it's not a spa. How does Sparkling Springs sound? It's a luxury spa hotel in the countryside, with an indoor heated pool, and views over the fields and woods nearby.
William:	That sounds exactly what I'm looking for. Let's go for that.
Travel Agent:	Excellent.

Questions 4–7
Track 41

Travel agent:	Now, if I can take some details, I can make the booking for you. Could I have your full name, please.
William:	Yup … my name's William French.
Travel agent:	William French … and your address?
William:	Number 4 The Willows, Standmarch, Norfolk, NE1 4SP.
Travel Agent:	The Willows. Sorry, how do you spell that?
William:	W-I-L-L-O-W-S. The Willows.
Travel Agent:	Thank you. And can I have a contact number for you?
William:	Yes. My mobile's probably the best one. It's 07632 112254.
Travel Agent:	07632 112250.
William:	No. It's 07632 112254.
Travel Agent:	Sorry, five four. And when would you like to go?
William:	On the weekend of the 15th June.
Travel Agent:	Fine. Checking in on 15th June. And when would you like to check out?
William:	I'd like to stay until the night of Monday 18th June. So I'd be leaving on Tuesday 19th.
Travel Agent:	Right. Check out on Tuesday 19th June. And how will you be paying?
William:	By credit card. How much will it be?
Travel Agent:	Ahhh. Let me see … four nights at ninety pounds per night is three hundred and sixty pounds. Is that OK?

| William: | It includes breakfast and dinner and a treatment a day. |
| | Yes. That sounds fine. I'm looking forward to it. |

Questions 8–10
Track 42

Travel Agent:	Would you like me to tell you how to get to the hotel once you're in the village? It's a bit difficult to find.
William:	Oh, yes, please. I have maps on my mobile phone, but there isn't always a signal.
Travel Agent:	OK. Well, coming in to the village from the motorway, which is in the east, the first building you see on your right is the church. It's right opposite the <u>garden centre</u>.
William:	OK. The church is on my right, and the garden centre on my left.
Travel Agent:	Yes … Just after that, you'll come to the railway crossing and then you'll see the river on your left. After that on the right you'll see the <u>school</u>. It's just before the bridge over the river.
William:	So the school's before the bridge.
Travel Agent:	Yes, that's right. Now just after the bridge, you'll see a turning on your left. Take that and follow the road through the fields. On your left, between the road and the river you'll see a lot of <u>vegetable</u> gardens. Just keep going down the road to the end. It leads straight into the car park at the <u>spa</u>. You can't miss it. It's at the end of the road.
William:	Thank you very much for your help.
Travel Agent:	My pleasure. I hope you have a lovely weekend.

Section 2
Questions 11–13
Track 43

Good morning. Welcome to the Science Museum. There's so much to do here, you could spend all day going from one exhibition to another. But if your time *is* limited, I'd suggest choosing maybe just one main exhibition. At the moment, I'd recommend our new exhibition of <u>everyday inventions</u>. It's amazing to see how objects we use in our daily lives, like paper clips, tea bags and light bulbs were invented in the first place and how they've developed over the years into such an essential part of our lives that we hardly ever notice them. You shouldn't miss it … The other thing I'd suggest if you don't have much time, is a guided tour of the free exhibitions. These tours usually start on the hour, umm … at one o'clock, two o'clock and so on. They're quite short, only <u>half an hour</u>, so you could do a couple of tours in an afternoon, if you wanted to. If you'd like to go on a tour, you should go to the entrance of the exhibition on the <u>ground floor</u> and wait for the guide there.

Questions 14–17
Track 44

Just to give you an idea of the range of exhibitions we have here at the museum, I'm going to tell you about the exhibitions and activities we have for visitors of different ages. First of all, for the <u>little ones</u>, we have a fascinating area called <u>Shapes and Patterns</u>, where they can play with objects and images and see how they form different patterns. It's really colourful and exciting. Kids love it. Then, at the other end of the scale we have more complex exhibitions that appeal more to our older visitors. There's one about the <u>history of aviation</u>, how planes developed over the years. Older visitors may even be able to remember some of the earlier planes on display. Another exhibition that adults might particularly enjoy is the <u>energy</u> exhibition. It shows the historical development of different forms of energy in Britain and how it has powered industry over the centuries. And, of course, we mustn't forget the <u>teenagers</u>. There are lots of exhibitions to interest them, but my favourite one is the one where visitors can find out more about how <u>physics</u> works. It's a fun exhibition with plenty of hands-on activities, that explore how light and heat and chemicals work. I still go there myself now and then. It's brilliant.

Questions 18–20
Track 45

Most of our exhibitions are free, but you will need a ticket for some of the special ones, like the 3D film shows. So let me explain how you get a ticket online. Of course, you can do this directly at the ticket office, but if there's a long queue, you can book online on your mobile. So, go to our home page and choose the 'events' button. Then click on the <u>film title</u>. That'll take you to the next window. In the right hand corner you'll see a little <u>calendar</u>. Choose the date on the calendar and then go to the next window. There's a drop down box there for you to choose the time and another one for the <u>number of tickets</u>. Careful on that page … there are different prices for adults and children. When you've done that, go to the final page and choose your payment method.

Section 3
Questions 21–23
Track 46

Tutor: So what's the survey about, Tom?

Tom: It's about where students want to live and how they choose. Basically, their accommodation preferences. We've actually tried it out with a few students, already.

Tutor: OK. That sounds fine. So to start with, how many questions have you got? Mmmm … 20?

Monica: Is that too many?

Tutor: Yes, it is, really. People get fed up answering lots of questions and they stop thinking about their answers.

Monica: Right, so we need to think about that again. What do you think of the first three questions?

Tutor: Ahmmm … You want to know what affects students' choice of accommodation when they go to university.

Monica: Yes. We want to find out which has the most effect: the cost, the number of rooms in the house or flat, or the distance from campus,

Tom: And then we asked another question.

Tutor: Oh, yes. What else did you want to find out?

Tom: Well, we wondered whether public transport was important. You know, not many students have cars. So it might be quite important for them to be near somewhere where they could catch a bus or train.

Tutor: Yeah, that's a good question.

Questions 24–26
Track 47

Tutor: Before you ask any more people, I've got a couple of suggestions for improving the questionnaire. First of all, I think you need to ask fewer questions. As I said, 20 is really too many. I'd cut it down to 10, if I were you.

Monica: OK, 10 questions only. And is there anything else you think we should do?

Tutor: Well, yes. Some of the questions are actually quite complicated. I think you should make them clearer. I mean, I think they should be easier to understand.

Monica: And, what do you think about asking more questions about cost?

Tutor: No. I don't think you need any more about cost. But you could ask a couple more questions about the reasons for students' decisions.

Monica: So we should ask some more questions with 'why'?'

Tutor: Yes. I think you'd get quite a lot more information if you did that.

Tom: Thank you.

Questions 27–30
Track 48

Tom: Ummm… we've already got some results from our first questionnaire. Do you think we could use them?

Tutor: I don't see why not. What have you found out so far?

Tom: Well, the number of rooms was only important for 16% of the people we asked. It looks like a lot of students are quite happy to share a room. And even fewer people were concerned about being near a bus stop, only 10%, in fact.

Tutor: I'm surprised about that. But what about the distance from the university?

Tom: Well, that was quite important. Around 20% of the students we asked wanted to be close to campus.

Tutor: Mmmm … that makes sense. And what about the cost?

Tom: Yeah, as we expected, the cost was by far the most important factor. More than half the students were concerned with the cost – 54% to be exact.

Tutor: Only 54%? … I thought it'd be closer to 80%!

Section 4
Questions 31–34
Track 49

My lecture this evening will focus on the migration of birds. That is, how birds fly in big groups from different parts of the world at certain times of the year. In the first part of the lecture I'll talk about the reasons why birds migrate, when they migrate and which parts of the world they migrate from and to. To start with, why do birds migrate? Well, there are two main reasons: One, they migrate to look for food and two, they travel to parts of the world that are more suitable for breeding. In fact, these reasons are closely linked. As you can imagine, when birds are breeding, they need extra food to feed their young. And, in the spring, in the cooler climates of

Europe, there is a lot of food for birds, especially insects. So, generally, during the spring, birds fly up from the tropics, which are hot, to cooler climates in the north. They stay there for a few months to bring up their young. And then when the weather in the north gets cold in the winter, they fly back to warmer climates in the south.

Questions 35–37
Track 50

Now I'd like to talk a bit about how global warming has affected bird migration. One of the effects of global warming has been to make the spring come earlier in the northern regions of the world. When spring comes early, the plants and insects that birds need to bring up their young are also available earlier. Research has shown that quite a lot of birds have started to migrate earlier, because of higher temperatures. But, unfortunately for some species, this hasn't been early enough. What I'm saying is that birds that are travelling a long way for breeding may arrive too late to find enough food to feed their young and their population drops drastically. Scientists are currently researching more about this.

Questions 38–40
Track 51

Now, I thought I'd finish by just briefly describing a few different patterns of migration. Ahhh … migration varies with the type of bird and the area they come from. For example, one kind of migration is 'partial' migration. This means that some birds in a particular species will migrate and others won't. It usually depends on how the weather affects food supplies and very often happens in the tropics. In another migratory pattern, a bird called an Arctic Tern migrates the whole length of the globe, from the north pole to the south. The Arctic Tern travels between twelve and fifteen thousand kilometres *each way* when it migrates in a complete circle around the world. It's quite amazing! Right … and, lastly, I'd like to mention a pattern which isn't nearly as spectacular, but is very interesting. And this is the way many birds migrate across North America. In this pattern the birds fly northwards in the west of the country and then back south again in the east. So, if you imagine it, they're actually migrating in a circular pattern, like the hands of a clock, not in a straight line, as we might think.

Answer key

Unit 1   Friends abroad

Part 1   Vocabulary

Exercise 1

a Japan

b Egypt

c Malaysia

d United Arab Emirates (UAE)

e Portugal

Exercise 2

1 Japanese

2 Chinese

3 Egyptian

4 Emirati

5 Portuguese

6 Malaysian

Exercises 3, 4

1 4.50

2 Beijing / China

3 UAE1880

4 Lisbon / Portugal

5 16

Part 2   Skills development

Exercise 1

1 6.50 p.m.

2 Wednesday 6th July

3 British Airways / BA3025

Exercise 2

13 – thirteen, 80 – eighty, 40 – forty, 15 – fifteen

Exercise 3

1 14

2 40

3 50

4 16.15

5 17.30

Exercise 4

i b

ii c

Exercise 5

1 3.30 a.m.

2 60

3 ABINGDON

4 OX14 3HB

5 612744

Exercise 6

1 HUA FANG

2 17 12 1994

3 13 PARK ROAD BRIGHTON, BN40 4GR

Part 3   Exam practice

1 Double – king-sized bed

2 Edward Francis

3 23 Cypress

4 CB3 9NF

5 taxi

6 breakfast

7 Friday 16th April

8 c

9 b

10 c

Unit 2   Food and cooking

Part 1   Vocabulary

Exercise 1

meat	dairy products	vegetables	fruit
lamb	cheese *butter*	potatoes	bananas
beef	milk	cabbage	pineapple
turkey	yoghurt	carrots	cherries

Exercise 2

2 U

3 C/U

4 C

5 U

6 C/U

7 U

8 C/U

9 C

10 C/U

Exercise 3

i D

ii E

iii A

iv C

v B

Exercise 4

1.3 **kg / kilos** of flour

20 *grams* of salt

300 **g / grams** of sugar

2 **l / litres** of milk

450 **ml / millilitres** of cooking oil

Exercise 5

1 ¾

2 two thirds

3 five eighths

4 ⅞

Exercise 6

1 ½ kilo – 500g

2 250g – ¼ kilo

3 330g – ⅓ kilo

4 200g – ⅕ kilo

5 ⅕l – 200ml

Part 2   Skills development

Exercise 1

2 c

3 d

4 a

5 h

6 g

Exercise 3

D, E, A, G, F, C, B

Exercise 4

1 *cut* the apples
2 (apples) with sugar
3 blackberries and apples
4 (a) baking dish
5 flour and butter (together)
6 (the) sugar
7 on top / on top of fruit
8 30 minutes

Exercise 5

1 deep fat   4 roast
2 healthy   5 vegetables
3 Friday night   6 at home

Part 3   Exam practice

1 eat properly   5–7 f, a, b
2 improving situation   8 government
3 right amount   9 schools
4 cereals *dairy foods* 10 families / parents

Unit 3   Presentations

Part 1   Vocabulary

Exercise 1

1 d   2 a   3 b   4 c

Exercise 2

2 presentation   present   present
3 suggest   suggestion
4 project   project   projector
5 inform   information
6 explain   explanation

Exercise 3

Farouk: So, who's going to do the introduction?
Edward: Well, I suggest you present the first part, Farouk. You've done a lot of work on this project, after all.
Farouk: Well, OK. I'll start. But you've got a lot of information, too. I think you should explain the next two slides.

Exercise 4

diagram: plan, graph, chart, table
picture: image, photograph, painting
language: French, Arabic, Chinese, Italian
advantages: pros, benefits, good points
disadvantages: bad points, dangers, cons

Part 2   Skills development

Exercise 1

i a   ii c   iii c   iv b

Exercise 2

1 a comparison   3 similar
2 8   4 different

Exercise 3

1 title box   3 image(s)
2 bullet points

Exercise 4

a, e

Part 3   Exam practice

Section 3

1–4
i b   ii c   iii b   iv b

5 Advantages
6 Accidents
7 Suggestions

8 Seven minutes
9 Two minutes
10 same style

Review 1

Exercise 1

/ei/	/iː/	/e/	/ai/	/iuː/
A	E	F	I	U
H	B	L	Y	Q
J	C	M		W
K	D	N		
	G	S		
	P	X		
	T	Z		
	V			

Exercise 2

1 British   4 arrival
2 departure   5 information
3 flight   6 connection

Exercise 3

1 onions
2 flour U
3 potatoes/U (e.g. mashed)
4 milk U
5 beans
6 cherries
7 coffee U
8 chicken(s)/U (food)

Exercise 4

1 one – ordinal numbers
2 ingredient – units of weight
3 dish – meals
4 who – sequence linking words
5 door – synonyms
6 wi-fi – places to eat
7 beans – drinks
8 pan – cooking methods
9 banana – vegetables
10 egg – dairy products

Exercise 5

1 The first thing we have to decide is our topic.
2 So, that's fixed then.
3 I think we should keep the blue bullet points.
4 I've put all our slides together.
5 So, let's put Botticelli first, and follow with Michelangelo.
6 Make sure all the slides have the same style.

Exercise 6

1 O	5 O	9 S
2 S	6 S	10 O
3 O	7 S	
4 O	8 S	

Unit 4   Work

Part 1   Vocabulary

Exercise 1
1 A = 3, B = 1, C = 4, D = 2

Exercise 2
1 businessman
2 police officer
3 doctor
4 farmer

Exercise 3
1 produce
2 supply, deliver
3 defend, guard
4 earn
5 trade
6 take care of

Exercise 4

1 look for
2 look after
3 look at
4 look over
5 look through

Exercise 5

1 look through
2 look for
3 look over
4 looked at
5 look after

Part 2   Skills development

Exercise 1
1 student societies
2 a large corporation
3 working outdoors
4 institutions of further education
5 job satisfaction
6 finding a job

Exercise 2
1 clubs, associations
2 company, business
3 in the open air, outside
4 colleges, universities
5 fulfilment, enjoyment
6 employment, work

Exercise 3
1 clubs
2 company
3 outside
4 universities
5 fulfilment
6 employment

Exercise 4

Alice:
1 a farm
2 fruit
3 chickens
4 (the) animals
5 summer
6 supermarkets
7 local shops
8 (the) public

Wei Long:
9 businessman
10 information technology
11 trade
12 small company
13 computer parts
14 receptionist
15 decisions
16 big company

Exercise 5
1 f   2 c   3 d

Part 3   Exam practice

1 police officer
2 law
3 practical
4 training

5–7 e, c, a
8 well-paid
9 famous people / celebrities
10 (a) detective

Unit 5 On campus services

Part 1 Vocabulary

Exercise 1
1 library
2 medical centre
3 sports centre
4 halls of residence

Exercise 2
1 sports centre
2 medical centre
3 sports centre
4 halls of residence (hall)

Exercise 3
1 through
2 There
3 restaurants
4 foreign
5 until
6 twelfth

Exercise 4
1 into
2 far away
3 outside
4 behind
5 between

Exercise 5
1 E
2 D
3 C
4 B
5 A

Part 2 Skills development

Exercise 1
1 the right
2 the corner
3 opposite
4 straight ahead of you
5 Medical Centre
6 to the lake

Exercise 2
1 of the wood
2 the first floor
3 round the lake
4 across the green
5 Student Union building
6 next

Exercise 3
1 ground floor
2 meet friends
3 first floor
4 on campus
5 four
6 play football

Exercise 4
1 D
2 A
3 B

Part 3 Exam practice

1 A
2 B
3 E
4 C
5 online catalogue
6 a number
7 plan
8 (student) ID card
9 makes a beep/
   sound / beeps
10 prints a ticket

Unit 6 Staying safe

Part 1 Vocabulary

Exercise 1
break into ✓, thief ✓, gun ✓, pickpocket ✓

Exercise 2

Noun	Verb	Adjective
crime	steal	dangerous
knife	rob	careful
gun	attack	safe
thief	protect	
gang	break into	
safe		

Exercise 3
1 burglar, stole (past tense)
2 pickpocket
3 shoplifter
4 gang, robbers (plural)
5 safe

Exercise 4
take to court
watch out for
call the police
lock up
crime scene

Exercise 5
1 broken into
2 called the police
3 crime scene
4 locked up
5 watch out for
6 take them to court

Exercise 7
When the receptionist arrived at Goodmead Primary School on Monday, she found that someone had broken into the office and stolen several laptops, so she called the police.

Part 2 Skills development

Exercise 1
1 What is the most common crime in the UK?
2 What two forms of theft does the policewoman mention?
3 Why are people in more danger when they are abroad?
4 What should people leave in the hotel on holiday?
5 What kind of mobile is popular with thieves?

Exercise 2
1 theft
2 robbery, burglary
3 (they) don't know country
4 passport and money
5 smart phone

Exercise 3
USA – 911, Australia – 000, Germany – 112, India – 100

Exercise 4
b

Exercise 5
i c   ii a   iii c   iv c

Part 3 Exam practice
1 India
2 handbag theft
3 Latin America
4 gun crime
5 expensive jewellery
6 lonely places
7 cash machines
8 c
9 b
10 b

Review 2

Exercise 1

Trade	Occupation	Education	Transport
business	doctor	graduated	truck
shop	nurse	studied	deliver
firm	rescue worker	university	supply
company	police officer		
	farmer		

Exercise 2
1 at
2 for
3 around
4 on
5 after, in

Exercise 3
1 accommodation
2 accident
3 library
4 opposite
5 business
6 Wednesday
7 February
8 necessary
9 relevant
10 responsible

Exercise 4
1 in, in
2 at
3 on / at, on
4 at
5 on
6 opposite, on

Exercise 5
1 Student union building
2 Library
3 Teaching block

Unit 7 Studying, exams and revision

Part 1 Vocabulary

Exercise 1
1 text books
2 test
3 exam hall
4 revision

Exercise 2

+ 'r'	+ 'er'	y + ier	more + adjective	irregular
later	faster	healthier	more interesting	worse
	slower	easier	more nervous	better
	cleverer			

Exercise 3
2 interesting   B
3 clever   C
4 nervous   B
5 slow   A
6 late   A
7 healthy   D
8 bad   E
9 good   E

Exercise 4
Suggested answers:
1 better
2 healthier
3 more interesting
4 slower
5 more nervous

Exercise 5
1 intelligent, correctly
2 well, effectively
3 fairly, quickly
4 unusually, good
5 extraordinarily, high

Part 2 Skills development

Exercise 1
1 b, d   2 c, d   3 a, c, d

Exercise 2
1 B   2 D   3 A   4 C

Exercise 3
1 revision timetable
2 in his mind
3 easier to concentrate
4 last-minute revision

Exercise 4
1 mobile (phone) in
2 in the doors
3 to the supervisor
4 examination number

Exercises 5, 6
1 F   3 A
2 E   4 C

Part 3 Exam practice

1 right exam paper
2 your examination number
3 the instructions
4 how long
5 several times
6 more difficult
7 know better
8 number of marks
9 (your) main ideas
10 a low mark

Unit 8 Shopping and spending

Part 1 Vocabulary

Exercise 1
a 2   c 4
b 1   d 3

Exercise 2
1 Ingrid complained to customer services about her new boots because the zip was broken.
2 A lot of teenagers like expensive designer brands more than cheap clothes.
3 One advantage of self-service is that you can choose your own food from the shelves.
4 Many young people in big cities go to shopping malls to meet their friends.
5 Farmers often sell their fruit and vegetables from market stalls.
6 The shop assistant helped the customer to find a T shirt in the colour they wanted.

Exercise 3
1 I bought this shirt in a sale.
2 My brother thinks online shopping is much quicker than going to the shops.
3 The good thing about shopping in a department store is that you can get everything in one place.
4 The last time I took something back to a shop, the customer services manager wasn't there.
5 I lost my credit card the other day. I was really worried someone else would use it.
6 Have you ever bought a train ticket with a student discount? It's so much cheaper.

Exercise 4
1 d   3 b   5 c
2 e   4 a

Exercise 5
1 go shopping
2 (shopping) list
3 supermarket
4 goes shopping
5 a refund

Part 2 Skills development

Exercise 1
2 then, next
3 secondly, finally
4 after, thirdly
5 lastly, prior to

Exercises 2a, b
1 75%
2 60%
3 50%
4 supermarkets
5 markets
6 small shops

Exercise 3
a, d, f

Exercise 4

1 a	3 f	5 c
2 e	4 d	6 b

Part 3   Exam practice

1 (more) mature people
2 spending patterns
3 up to 30
4 over 55
5–7 f, a, d
8 cars and computers
9 beauty treatments
10 young men

Unit 9   Hobbies, interests and sports

Part 1   Vocabulary

Exercise 1

Hobby	Interest	Sport
4 stamp collecting	2 going to the cinema/ movies	1 cycling
5 painting	3 playing video games	6 basketball

Exercise 2

Hobbies	Interests	Sports
stamp collecting	going to the cinema	cycling
painting	playing chess	basketball
gardening	travelling	swimming
cooking	listening to music	running
	going to art galleries	football

Exercise 3

A 1 swimming
  2 running
B 1 cinema
  2 concert
C 1 travelling
  2 gardening
D 1 cycling
  2 cooking

Exercise 4

1 to	3 two	5 to
2 too	4 too	6 two

Part 2   Skills development

Exercise 1

1 fry
2 pray
3 lead
4 blade
5 correct
6 play
7 read
8 fly
9 played
10 collect

Exercise 2

1 flying	2 play	3 leading

Exercise 3

1 number
2 date
3 name of country

Exercise 4

1 1998	3 1967
2 USA/United States	4 Brazil

Exercise 5

2 address
3 name/spelling
4 phone number
5 personal/medical information
6 personal history

Exercise 6

1 Andrew Metcalfe
2 21
3 43A
4 571324
5 some

Part 3   Exam practice

1 table tennis
2 100
3 12
4 street dance
5–7 e, b, g
8 Mandeville
9 Bury Gardens
10 573279

Review 3

Exercise 1

1 easier	3 toughest	5 better
2 longer	4 worst	6 best

Exercise 2

2 prettier
3 cleverer
4 better
5 more difficult
6 healthier
7 nearer
8 harder
9 earlier
10 more boring

Exercise 3

Shop	Discount	Fashion	Goods
store	bargain	style	items
supermarket	deal	design	produce
market	reduction		articles
	sale price		

Exercise 4

1 young men
2 eating out
3 improving home(s)

Exercise 5

1 two people, where, going on holiday, complete the sentences, NO MORE THAN TWO WORDS OR A NUMBER
2 how to join a club, complete the form, TWO WORDS
3 two students, hobbies, complete the notes, NO MORE THAN THREE WORDS OR A NUMBER
4 woman, friend, weekend, match the woman's opinion, activities
5 two people, favourite film, choose correct answer, list (A-C)

Exercise 6

2	3	4	5
dates ages prices names phone numbers times addresses activities days sports	comparisons activities days sports hobbies	comparisons weather times activities days sports cities hotels hobbies	comparisons stories actors names types of film

Unit 10   Work-life balance

Part 1   Vocabulary

Exercise 1
Suggested answers:
1 stress
2 deadline
3 relaxation
4 employer

Exercise 2
1 hobby
2 work
3 comfort
4 beach
5 worker
6 start

Exercise 3

Noun	Noun and verb
career	rest
job	work
hobby	stress
profession	worry
occupation	comfort
relaxation	shop
leisure	boss
difficulty	start
	pressure

Exercise 4
1 job
2 holidays
3 worry
4 office
5 owner
6 deadline

Exercise 5
1 New York is not the capital of the United States of America.
2 In the UK, children who are born in July usually start school in September, just after they are five.
3 Oxford University is one of the most famous in the world.
4 In some countries, most companies close on Sundays, but in other countries they close on Fridays or Saturdays.
5 The official language of Greece is Greek.

Part 2   Skills development

Exercise 1
ii Their holidays start at the beginning of July.

Exercise 2
i b   ii a   iii b   iv b

Exercise 3
1 nine/9, five/5
2 come into
3 don't have
4 On Mondays
5 come out

Exercise 4
A 3   D 1   G 2
B 7   E 6
C 4   F 5

Exercise 5
1 B   3 F   5 A
2 E   4 G

Part 3   Exam practice

1 and mental
2 private
3 flexible
4 from home
5 a year
6 job sharing
7 27%
8 work from home
9 two small children
10 her sister's

Unit 11   Comparing cultures

Part 1   Vocabulary

Exercise 1

Across:	Down:
3 national	1 Chinese
4 huts	2 Italy

Exercise 2

1 pronunciation	5 scarf
2 alphabet	6 silk
3 spicy	7 brick
4 vegetarian	8 block of flats

Exercise 3
1 diet
2 housing
3 communication
4 costume

Exercise 4
1 spicy
2 blocks of flats
3 language, alphabet
4 silk

Exercise 5

1 have	4 had
2 made	5 do
3 done	6 have

Part 2   Skills development

Exercise 1

the same as	more [common] than
much more [open]	[friendlier] than
in comparison with	

Exercise 2

To emphasize similarity	To limit similarity
very	a bit
extremely	rather
incredibly	quite
exactly	not
	a little

Exercise 3

1 f	2 e	3 d

Exercise 4
1 In traditional Indian families, where did the bride and groom use to meet for the first time?
2 In India, what did the father of the bride use to do?
3 What has it become popular for Indian families to do recently?
4 Where does the couple live after they are married?

Exercise 5

i b	ii c	iii a	iv b

Part 3   Exam practice

1 b	6 water festivals
2 b	7 six
3 a	8 life, wealth, luck
4 e	9 new year
5 g	10 (by) ancient tradition

Unit 12   Exploring the oceans

Part 1   Vocabulary

Exercise 1
Suggested answers:

Picture 1	Picture 2	Picture 3	Picture 4
oil rig	gas pipeline	fishing trawler	underwater turbine *
off-shore drilling	natural gas	net	wave power
mineral resource	mineral resource	fish farm	energy
fuel	fuel		
natural gas			

Exercise 2

1 f	3 d	5 c
2 e	4 b	6 a

Exercise 3

1 source	3 affected	5 break
2 sea	4 Our	6 currents

Exercise 4
The graphs show trends.

1 d	2 a	3 b	4 c

Exercise 5

Suggested answers:

Statistics	Trends
average (noun/adjective)	rise (noun/verb)
majority (noun)	fall (noun/verb)
minority (noun)	increase (noun/verb)
less than (adjective)	decrease (noun/verb)
more than (adjective)	remain stable (verb + adverb)
fraction (noun)	downward (adverb/adjective)
number (noun)	upward (adverb/adjective)
per cent (noun)	tendency (noun)
amount (noun)	dramatic (adjective)
significant (adjective)	gradual (adjective)
slight (adjective)	

Part 2   Skills development

Exercise 1

1 underwater (sub = under, marine = sea)
2 not deep (fixed rigs need to rest on the sea bed)
3 fish farming (aqua = water/culture = growing)
4 journey down (to the ocean floor), shown
   (has + verb), marine (= sea)

Exercise 2

Noun	Adjective	Verb
Aquaculture	submarine	revealed
descent	shallow	
	marine	

Exercise 3

1 derrick
2 helicopter pad
3 support tower
4 crane

Exercise 4

1 2008 = 4
2 2009 = 2
3 2012 = 18
4 2014 = 60

Part 3   Exam practice

1 1000 metres
2 1940s
3 1960
4 11,000 metres
5 pilot's
6 batteries
7 panel of lights
8 fin
9 surface of earth
10 minerals for industry

Review 4

Exercise 1

1 Is gardening a hobby or a sport?
2 Several thousand people ran in the London
   Marathon in 2012.
3 South America is a very large continent with a
   variety of climates.
4 In many large companies employees work
   from Monday to Friday, and some even work on
   Saturdays.
5 Hindi is the official language of India.
6 An Australian accent is not the same as a New
   Zealand one.
7 The capital of the United States is not New York,
   but Washington D.C.
8 Oxford University is one of the best in the world.

Exercise 2

1 studies
2 thank
3 languages
4 classes
5 countries
6 communication

Exercise 3

1 make
2 have
3 do
4 have
5 have
6 made
7 have
8 have

Exercise 4

1 more beautiful than
2 easier, the same as
3 greasier than
4 much more exciting
   than
5 as hot as
6 more conservative than
7 as cold as

Exercise 5

1 Currants
2 sea
3 affected
4 accept
5 Except
6 source
7 currents
8 descent

Exercise 6

Noun	Adjective	Verb	Adverb
majority	marine	hatch	scientifically
descent	submarine *	descend	significantly
submarine *	shallow	explore	gradually
exploration	mysterious	research *	
research *	technologically	reveal	
scientist			
technology			
mystery			
revelation			

Practice test

Section 1

1 a
2 b
3 a
4 4, The Willows
5 07632 112254
6 19th June
7 £360
8 garden centre
9 school
10 vegetable

Section 2

11 Everyday inventions
12 half an hour
13 ground floor
14 c
15 b
16 B
17 A
18 film title
19 calendar
20 number of tickets

Section 3

21 (student) accommodation
22 distance from campus
23 public transport
24 e
25 b
26 f
27 16%
28 near bus stop
29 20%
30 54%

Section 4

31 look for food
32 feed their young/find extra food
33 the tropics
34 warmer climates
35 it comes earlier
36 higher temperatures
37 (it) drops drastically
38 D
39 F
40 B

Glossary

Key

abbr. = abbreviation
adj. = adjective
adv. = adverb
n. = noun
phrasal v. = phrasal verb
phr. = phrase
v. = verb

Unit 1

arrival **n.** – the act or time of arriving
available **adj.** – If something is available you can have or use it.
book **v.** – to reserve a seat on a flight, room in a hotel, etc.
departure **n.** – the act or time of leaving
get in **v.** – to arrive, especially at one's home or place of work
land **v.** – When a plane lands, it comes down to the ground after a flight.
pick-up point **n.** – a place to collect passengers, goods, etc.
terminal **n.** – the building where people wait at an airport or to catch a ferry
travel agent **n.** – someone whose job is to arrange holidays for people

Unit 2

amount **n.** – The amount of something is how much there is or how much you need.
balanced diet **n.** – a diet that contains enough of the necessary nutrients for you to be healthy
benefit **n.** – something good that you get from something
boil **v.** – to cook food in very hot water
boiling **adj.** – very hot
bowl **n.** – a round container open at the top, used for holding liquid, keeping fruit, serving food, etc.
cabbage **n.** – a large, round vegetable with white, green or purple leaves that is usually eaten cooked

canteen **n.** – a restaurant in a factory, school, etc. where workers, students, etc. eat
cauliflower **n.** – a large, round vegetable with a white centre surrounded by green leaves, which is eaten cooked
crumble **n.** – a baked pudding consisting of a crumbly mixture of flour, fat and sugar over stewed fruit
dish **n.** – food that is prepared and cooked in a particular way
eighth **n.** – one of eight equal parts of something
flavour **n.** – the taste of a food or drink
flip **v.** – to turn something over with a sudden quick movement
fry **v.** – to cook food in very hot fat or oil
get straight on (with) **v.** – to do something with no delay
grease **v.** – If you grease a cooking dish, you put a thin layer of fat on it to stop food from sticking to it when cooking.
greasy **adj.** – coated with or full of grease
grill **v.** – to cook meat, fish, etc. by direct heat, as under a grill or over a hot fire
half **n.** – one of two equal parts of something
lamb **n.** – the meat of a young sheep
measures **n.** – particular actions intended to achieve something
melted **adj.** – Something that is melted has become a liquid because of heat.
mix **v.** – to combine liquids, substances, etc. together
packet food **n.** – food that is quick and easy to prepare, e.g. food that is precooked
peel **v.** – to remove the skin or outer covering of fruit, vegetables or eggs
pineapple **n.** – a tropical fruit with yellow flesh and a hard brown skin that has sharp points on it
quarter **n.** – one of four equal parts of something
recipe **n.** – a list of ingredients and instructions that tell you how to cook something
roast **v.** – to cook meat or vegetables by dry heat, usually with added fat and especially in an oven
rub (in) **v.** – to mix fat into flour using your fingers to get a crumbly mixture
solve **v.** – to find the solution to a problem
spice **n.** – a plant or powder from a plant that you add to food to give it flavour, e.g. ginger, cinnamon or nutmeg
steam **v.** – to cook food with steam from hot water

stir **v.** – to use a spoon to mix a liquid or other substance

syrup **n.** – a sweet, thick, sticky liquid

take measures **v.** – to take actions to achieve a particular goal

third **n.** – one of three equal parts of something

tiny **adj.** – very small

Unit 3

ceiling **n.** – the top inside surface of a room

concentrate on **v.** – to focus all attention on a particular thing you are doing

explain **v.** – to give details about something so that people can understand

fair enough **phr.** – an expression of agreement

for instance **phr.** – for or as an example

introduce **v.** – to speak at the beginning of a presentation, television programme, etc. and tell people what they are going to see or hear

make sense **v.** – If something makes sense, it is reasonable or sensible.

make sure **v.** – to make certain

match **v.** – to be the same or similar and look good together

memory stick **n.** – a small object that you can carry and use for storing information from a computer, digital camera, etc.

present **v.** – to give information to people, e.g. in a presentation or speech

project **v.** – to make an image appear on a surface

pros and cons **phr.** – the advantages and disadvantages of something

rob **v.** – to steal something from someone, especially in a violent way

slide **n.** – a small piece of film in a frame, that you can see on a screen using a special piece of equipment

suggest **v.** – to put forward a plan or idea for someone to think about

Unit 4

arrest **v.** – If the police arrest someone, they take the person to a police station because they think the person has committed a crime.

avoid **v.** – to prevent something bad from happening

baby-sitter **n.** – a person who takes care of a child or children while the parents are out

career **n.** – a job or profession

celebrity **n.** – a famous person

close up **adv.** – If you see someone or something close up, you are near them and can see them very well.

deliver **v.** – to take goods to a place

earn **v.** – to get money in return for work

feed **v.** – to give food to

fulfilment **n.** – the feeling of achieving something important or desired

guard **v.** – to watch a person or thing in order to protect them

join **v.** – to become a member of a club, organization, etc.

load **v.** – to put goods onto a truck, ship, etc.

open air **n.** – The open air is any place outside.

police force **n.** – an organization of police officers in a particular country or area

rep. **abbr. n.** – abbreviation for a person that represents someone else

reward **n.** – something you get because you have worked or done something good

stressful **adj.** – involving or causing mental or emotional pressure or worry

supply **v.** – to provide something

treatment **n.** – medicine, surgery, etc. that someone is given if they are ill or injured

union representative **n.** – someone who represents a group of students or workers

Unit 5

borrow **v.** – to take or use something for a period of time and then give it back

concentrate **v.** – to focus all attention on a particular thing you are doing

custom **n.** – an activity or way of behaving that is usual or traditional in a particular place

food hall **n.** – the part of a department store, where food is sold

food outlet **n.** – a place that sells food

footpath **n.** – a narrow path for people to walk on

foreign **adj.** – coming from or relating to another country

get cash out **v.** – to get money from a machine or bank

journal **n.** – a newspaper or magazine, especially one that deals with a particular subject

lecture **n.** – a talk that is given to students to teach them

lecture theatre **n.** – a large room or hall with seats in tiers where students sit to listen to lectures

lift **n.** – something that carries people up and down in a tall building

lobby **n.** – the room at the entrance of a large building such as a hotel

owe **v.** – If you owe someone some money, you need to pay it to them.

pastry **n.** – an individual cake or pastry pie

path **n.** – a long strip of ground for people to walk on from one place to another

round **adj.** – in the shape of a circle

stir-fry **n.** – a Chinese dish made by cooking small pieces of meat and vegetables in very hot oil

students' union building **n.** – the building where the organization that helps students has its offices, and which usually also has a bar, shops, etc.

take out **v.** – to borrow a book from a library

tough **adj.** – difficult

upset **v.** – to make someone feel unhappy

Unit 6

abroad **adv.** – to or in a foreign country

advise **v.** – to tell someone what you think they should do

break into **v.** – to go into a house or other building illegally in order to steal something

burglar **n.** – someone who enters a building illegally in order to steal things

cash machine **n.** – a machine where you go to get money

catch **v.** – to find and stop someone who is trying to escape

crime **n.** – an illegal action that someone can be punished for

get through to (on the phone) **phrasal v.** – to be connected to someone on the telephone

grab **v.** – to take something with force

handbag **n.** – a bag that a woman carries to hold her purse, keys, etc.

lock up **v.** – to lock the doors and windows of a building before you leave

lonely **adj.** – A lonely place is a long way from other places and very few people go there.

pickpocket **n.** – a person who steals from the pockets or handbags of others in public places

ring **v.** – to call someone using a telephone

rob **v.** – If someone is robbed, someone steals something from them.

safe **n.** – a strong, metal container with special locks, used for storing money, jewellery and other valuable objects

shoplifter **n.** – a person who steals things from a shop by hiding them in a bag or in clothes

steal **v.** – to take something without someone's permission

stranger **n.** – any person who you do not know

take someone to court **v.** – to start a legal process against someone

theft **n.** – the crime of stealing something

watch out for **v.** – to pay attention so that you will see someone or something

Unit 7

be worth **v.** – to have a particular value or price

blank **adj.** – If your mind goes blank, you cannot think of anything or remember anything.

calm down **v.** – to begin to feel less worried, nervous, upset, etc.

download **v.** – to copy something to your computer using the Internet

extraordinarily **adv.** – extremely and unusually

keep your eye on the clock **v.** – to be aware of the time so that you are not late or so that you finish something on time

locker **n.** – a small cupboard with a lock that you can put your bags, valuable objects, etc. in at school

revision **n.** – the process of rereading a subject or notes on it, especially in preparation for an examination

roughly **adv.** – without being exact

several **determiner** – more than a few

software **n.** – the programs that can be used by computers for doing particular jobs

try out **v.** – to use a method to find out if it is successful

Unit 8

boutique **n.** – a shop, especially a small one selling fashionable clothes

brand **n.** – a particular product or products with a trade name or trademark

complain **v.** – to say that you are not satisfied with something

department store **n.** – a large shop divided into different parts that each sell different things

discount **n.** – a reduction in the usual price of something

eat out **v.** – to eat away from home, especially in a restaurant

grocery shopping **n.** – shopping for food

household goods **n.** – the things you use in your house

mature adult **n.** – an old person, used as a way of avoiding saying the word 'old'

on the spur of the moment **adv.** – If you do something on the spur of the moment, you suddenly decide to do it and do not plan it.

organic **adj.** – grown without the use of chemicals

outing **n.** – a short trip to a place

refund **n.** – an amount of money that a shop gives back to you because you have bought something that you are not satisfied with

sale **n.** – a time when a shop sells things at less than their usual price

self-service **adj.** – A self-service restaurant, shop, machine, etc. is one where you get something for yourself and people do not bring it to you.

shelves **n.** – the flat pieces of wood, metal or glass that things are displayed on in a shop

spending habits **n.** – Your spending habits are the types of things that you usually buy, where you buy them, how much you spend, etc.

survey **n.** – a set of questions that you ask a large number of people or organizations

take something back **v.** – to return goods to a shop

trip **n.** – a journey or visit to a place

zip **n.** – something that opens and closes clothes and bags. It has two rows of metal or plastic teeth and you pull something along them.

Unit 9

climb **v.** – to use your hands and feet to go up rocks as a sport

cross country **adj.** – going across countryside, as opposed to tracks or roads

join **v.** – to become a member of a club, organization, etc.

keen on **adj.** – If you are keen on something, you like it.

lazy **adj.** – not wanting to work

leisure **n.** – the time when you are not working and can relax and enjoy yourself

marathon **n.** – a race on foot of 26 miles 385 yards (42,195 kilometres)

membership fee **n.** – a charge made for being a member of an organization

parrot **n.** – a brightly coloured bird that can sometimes copy what people say

stamp **n.** – the thing that you stick on an envelope or parcel to show that you have paid to post it

street dance **n.** – a dance style that started outside of dance studios in any open spaces such as streets, parks, school yards, etc.

Unit 10

accounting **n.** – the department in charge of keeping financial accounts

alert **v.** – to tell someone about something or remind them about something

deadline **n.** – a time limit for any activity

draft **n.** – an early version of a letter, report, etc. that you might change later

draw the line **v.** – to make a distinction between two things and consider them as being separate

enter (data) **v.** – to write or key information in a computer

human resource manager **n.** – the person in charge of the department that interviews, appoints or keeps records of employees in an organization

manage your money **v.** – to spend your money carefully so that you do not waste it and so that you have enough for the things you need

milestone **n.** – a significant event that marks an important stage in a process *nursery* **n.** – a school for young children, usually from three to five years old

on the dot **phr.** – at exactly the arranged time

outline **n.** – a general plan or description of something, without the exact details

part-time **adj.** – Part-time work is work in which you only work for part of each day or week.

phase **n.** – a particular stage in a process, project, etc.

pick up **v.** – to collect someone and take them somewhere

pressure **n.** – a worried feeling that you get because you have to do a lot of things in a short time or because people expect a lot from you

questionnaire **n.** – a set of written questions that are sent to a lot of people in order to get information

stress **n.** – a feeling of being worried or tense

task **n.** – an activity or piece of work that you have to do

timetable **n.** – a list of your lessons and when they will happen

worry **n.** – a feeling of being anxious because of problems you have or because of what might happen

Unit 11

arrange **v.** – to make plans or preparations for something to happen

block of flats **n.** – a building that contains apartments

bride **n.** – a woman who has just been or is about to be married

chat **v.** – to have an informal conversation

cotton **n.** – cloth made from fibre from a cotton plant

do damage **v.** – to cause physical harm to something

festival **n.** – a day or period when people in a place celebrate a special event

global warming **n.** – an increase in the average temperature worldwide believed to be caused by the greenhouse effect

groom **n.** – a man who has just been or is about to be married

lentils **n.** – small seeds from a lentil plant which can be cooked and eaten in soups and stews

make progress **v.** – to advance, to get results

origins **n.** – The origins of something are where it came from and how it started to exist.

splash **v.** – If you splash someone with water, you move your hands and feet in water so that the other person gets water on themselves.

Unit 12

at risk – If something bad is at risk of happening, it is likely to happen.

behaviour **n.** – the way that someone behaves

chamber **n.** – a room equipped for a particular purpose

crane **n.** – a device for lifting and moving heavy objects

current **n.** – a steady, flowing movement of water

decrease **v.** – to become less

descend **v.** – to move downwards

destructive **adj.** – causing damage

drill turbine **n.** – a machine with a rotating tool for boring cylindrical holes

fall **v.** – to become less or lower in number, quality, price, etc.

fin **n.** a thin, flat part out that sticks out of a rocket, submarine, etc. and helps to control its movement

float **v.** – If something floats, it stays on the surface of water and does not sink.

fuel **n.** – any substance burned as a source of heat or power, such as coal or petrol

gas pipeline **n.** – a long pipe, especially underground, used to transport natural gas over long distances

generate **v.** – to produce a form of energy or power

globe **n.** – the world

gradual **adj.** – happening slowly

helicopter pad **n.** – a place for helicopters to land and take off

ice-cap **n.** – a thick layer of ice that covers the North and South Poles

increase **v.** – to become bigger in size or number

manned **adj.** – A manned ship, spacecraft, etc. has people in it who are operating its controls.

melt **v.** – If something solid melts, it becomes a liquid because of heat.

off-shore **adj.** – done or happening in the sea

oil platform **n.** – a large structure that stands on the seabed, used for getting oil from under the sea

oil rig **n.** – a structure on land or in the sea, that is used for getting oil or gas from under the ground

pilot **n.** – a person who is steering a ship or submarine *power* **n.** – a particular form of energy

prawn **n.** – a small shellfish with a long tail and a lot of legs, which you can eat

renewable **adj.** – Renewable energy forms are natural ones which will always be available, e.g. wind.

resource **n.** – something such as a material or money that a country or organization has and can use

reveal **v.** – to show that something exists

rise **v.** – to increase in height or level

sample **n.** – a small amount of something that is taken and tested scientifically

sea bed **n.** – the ground at the bottom of the sea

shallow **adj.** – Shallow water is not very deep.

significant **adj.** – big enough to be important

stable **adj.** – not changing

storm **n.** – an occasion when there is very heavy rain and strong winds, and sometimes thunder and lightning

structure **n.** – something that has been built from parts, especially a large building

surface **n.** – the top level of the land or sea

tendency **n.** – something that is starting to happen more often

trawler **n.** – a boat used for catching fish, which has a wide net that is pulled behind the boat

trend **n.** – a change or development towards something different

upward **adj.** – moving towards a higher point or level

wave **n.** – *(in sea)* a raised mass of water on the surface of the sea caused by the wind or by tides making the surface of the water rise and fall

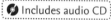
  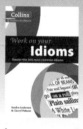